Baby Boomers' Official Guide to Retirement Income

Over 100 part-time or seasonal start-up businesses for the new retiree

By Stan Spector

© 2007 Stan Spector
All Rights Reserved.

No part of this publication may be reproduced, stored in a retrieval system, or transmitted, in any form or by any means, electronic, mechanical, photocopying, recording, or otherwise, without the written permission of the author.

First published by Dog Ear Publishing
4010 W. 86th Street, Ste H
Indianapolis, IN 46268
www.dogearpublishing.net

ISBN: 978-159858-342-7

This book is printed on acid-free paper.

Printed in the United States of America

This book was presented to

by

Table of Contents

Introduction

Why this book 1
Why you may have a "sustainable competitive advantage" 3
Types of businesses we are talking about 5
Who are the right people to start a business? 9
Those required skills 11
Franchises 13
MLM Multilevel Marketing or Network Marketing 15
Financing your business 17
Working Capital 19
Traits to look for in your business 21
Other benefits 23
Exit Strategy 25
Business Reference Material 27
Due Diligence 29
A few warnings 31
Mini-Business Plan 33

Opportunities

Business Opportunity Listings 35
Advocate 37
After-school activities for students 38
Antique Dealer/Restoring 38
Auto detailing and doll up 39
Bar-B-Q caterer 40
Bartending 41
Bed and Breakfast 41

Brokering 42
Business center for a captive audience 43
Caravan guide 44
Card maker 44
Cash/Coin Operated Businesses 45
Catering and private chef 46
Christmas decorator 47
Coaching 48
Coffee Carts 48
College bound student's services 49
College campus publication 49
Concierge 50
Concrete coatings 51
Consulting 52
Contractor referral service 52
Coupon books 53
Coupon mailings 54
Courier 55
Cruise experts/speakers 55
Data Mining 56
Digital Keepsakes 57
Disposables sales 58
Document destruction 58
Document preservation-Personal 59
Dog Kennels 60
Elderly moving 61
Elderly services 62
Embroidery 62
Ethnic or geographic publications 63
Expense Reduction Analyst 63
Fall cleanup aide 64
Fence and mailbox installer 65
Festival Organizer 65
Financial planning 66
Fitness and health products 67
Floral Preservation 68

Food preparation for specialty diets 68
Food Stands 69
Fractional Ownership 69
Fun Education 70
Fundraising Packager 71
Garden curbs 71
Garden Products 72
Geocaching Games 73
Gift Baskets for Special Occasions 73
Hobby finished products 74
Hobby supplies 75
Holiday items 75
Home delivery of heavy products 76
Home-made food products 76
Home spring cleaning 77
House sitter 77
House swap coordinator 78
How-to videos 79
Ice cream shop 79
Industrial equipment maintenance 80
Inflatables 80
Information centers/kiosk 81
International flight courier 82
Janitorial 82
Jewelry sales 83
Liquidators of personal property 83
Mail, re-mail, internal mail sorting and fulfillment services . . .84
Marketing for small companies 85
Medical Auditor 85
Mobile oil change 86
Mold testing 87
Non-medial services for elderly, disabled or busy patrons 87
Old fashion skills 88
On-site computer support 88
Opener/closer 89
Organizers 89

Outdoor activities	90
Pamphlet publishing	91
Party host	91
Personal trainer/Fitness trainer	92
Plants, flowers or vegetables	93
Plant renter	93
Poster/Picture Renter	94
Printer Cartridge Refill	94
Product packager	95
Publish your own book	96
Recognition awards/custom imprinting	97
Rock Hound	97
Safety and security equipment for home and small business	98
Seafood truck sales	99
Self-Storage	100
Seminar host	101
Sewing Services	101
Sign shop in your basement	102
Small motor and equipment repair	102
Snowplowing	103
Specialized car mechanic	104
Specialty industrial customer newsletter	104
Specialty industrial newsletter	105
Specialty tools	105
Spring cleanup aide	106
Spring flower garden design and plantings	106
Summer food sales	107
Summer recreational equipment rentals	107
Tax preparation	108
Telephone surveyor	108
Theme publication	109
Tourists' maps	110
Tutoring	110
Utility Auditor	111
Valentine Day stores	111

Vending routes 112
Videographer 112
Water purification equipment 113
Web sales 114
Wine tasting 114
Wine Tours 115
Winter motorized equipment rental 115
Winter recreational equipment rentals 116
Wood-lot management 116

Why this book

Baby boomers, as they approach retirement age, have heard about the changing face of retirement. No longer will they be able to take their social security check, a modest company retirement plan and limited retirement savings and move down to Florida, spend their days golfing at private country clubs or fishing from their 40 foot cruiser, traveling to exotic places in the world for vacations, eating out every night (even if it is the discounted early bird specials) and living in a nice but modest house. For a few, this might be what their retirement looks like.

But many will decide, by choice, that this life is not for them. Others, who do not have sufficient financial resources, will out of necessity of getting by day-to-day have a different lifestyle. No matter what the reason is, many will have to find full-time or supplementary jobs or businesses to operate during their golden years. I call this change in the golden years, new-tirement.

You may have a current job that you really like that you can take with you into retirement, either through working part time, a portion of the year or as a consultant. If you really enjoy your work and are willing to continue, this will probably be your best opportunity to maximize your income and/or minimize your time devoted to work. The higher the skill level your work requires, the more experience required or the more complex the experience, the more this type of retirement will meet your financial goals.

But others will not be able to do this or will choose to move into a more enjoyable job or business, deciding to follow their dreams and not the money. For those of you who choose this path, this book is written to provide you some guidance and some reference material.

Why you may have a "sustainable competitive advantage"

If you start a business and write a business plan to apply for a bank loan, the first question you may be asking is what is the "sustainable competitive advantage" that you have that will allow your business to succeed over the competition

A competitive advantage is why people will buy your product or service instead of the competition. It may be that your product or service is unique from what the competition is selling. If it is, a portion of the customers may prefer your product and buy from you. It may be your location. If you are located where people will be using your product, you have an advantage over competition not located where you are. If you are at a high traffic location, people may decide on the spur of the moment to buy what you are selling. Even if there is competition nearby, you may get a portion of the business. This is common with food items at a festival or beach. You may also be able to produce and sell your product or service at a lower price than the competition. Some of the customers are price sensitive and will use a lower priced option for the same product. You may gain this cost advantage by reducing overhead costs such as not paying rent for the use of your basement, yard or equipment to run the business. It may be that you can afford to pay yourself less to work in your business as long as you can work at your own convenience.

But is your competitive advantage sustainable? Will some major store start producing a knock off of your product? Will a discount store start selling it cheaper by having their product manufactured in a foreign country that pays the workers $1 per day? You may have some barrier to entry that the competition cannot overcome as cheaply as you do or do not see a large enough market to make it worth their entering the business. Location specific businesses have an advantage but if competition sees you making lots of money, they will start up right next to you.

Sustainable competitive advantage may be hard to define but if you have one, you will know it.

Types of businesses we are talking about

I will go into more specific ideas later but I do want to plant some categories in your mind so you will be thinking about what you could do as you read the rest of this book.

1. **Hobby businesses** Many people think of these businesses first for supplemental income. The vision is doing something for cash that you have been paying to do in the past for fun. This is a lot of people's dream for retirement. These businesses frequently don't do well as a full time job. There may be a lot of other people that have the same hobby that will enter the same business as you have chosen when they try to retire. Consider selling supplies for this hobby or making end products for sale and allowing a retailer to sell the product for you. Building wood bridges for gardens or Adirondack chairs would be a good business for someone whose hobby is woodworking. Your product should be different from the competition's product and although you might only sell a few each year, some local garden shop may want to put some of your products on their property in their displays and sell them for you.

2. **Seasonal businesses** There are a number of businesses that only work during certain seasons. Businesses like cross country skis or snowshoe rentals at a local park, ice cream sales, motor boat rentals or beach chair rentals at the water's edge, are a few. You can't make a full paycheck from these businesses in many parts of the country but you can make quite a lot of money during the key months.

3. **Festival businesses** Every summer there are thousands of outdoor festivals with people selling bottled condiments, kettle corn, all kinds of foods, soaps and scented plant mixes. If you talk to these people, you will find that many are on a circuit and do 20 to 30 weekend festivals each year. Depending on their product and quality, they can be making little money but have a fun lifestyle for themselves or they can be making quite a lot of money. I once ran into a person who was selling a product at these sales. He had a Ph.D. and had taught for years at a college. He tried to sell his product one summer when he needed some extra money. Now he does it full time and makes more money than he made as a college professor. You might even want to be a festival planner for a specific type of festival. I have heard of some people making a very nice profit from running only one festival a year.

4. **Vending routes** Hard work and heavy lifting are often associated with vending machines. No retiring person should be considering loading soda machines 8 hours every day. There is plenty of competition in the food areas. But there is a whole other world of vending of rare items or vending to captive audiences. Growing and selling worms from cooler-type vending machines in high traffic fishing boat launch areas can be a great business. I have been shocked at how much some gumball routes make when they charge $.25 a gumball. The hard part of many of these businesses is getting the machines in good locations, which takes time, perseverance and good salesmanship skills.

5. **Excess Assets** Some businesses use "excess" assets. This may involve using your 1/8 acre back yard to grow plants. You can use your yard free of charge to your business but a commercial grower would have to pay rent and taxes for their yard space. Later in this book, you will see an example of a website that instructs you how to start a mini-nursery in your yard.

If you have a fairly empty basement in your house, you might be able to use it for storage, sorting of mail, assembling items or imprinting materials; commercial businesses pay high rents for comparable space.

Many businesses have to pay more for certain services than homeowners do. Long distance phone service can be purchased for your home office on an unlimited basis for a very modest sum. But businesses pay a lot more for long distance and local phone service. Home businesses utilizing this type of discounted residential services for surveys and information gathering can have a sustainable competitive advantage and can be very profitable for a supplemental business as long as these home-office uses are allowed.

Who are the right people to start a business?

First of all, you must be a self-starter. If you were a worker in your working years and performed the specific tasks that someone else requested, you might not be the right person. Starting a business is hard, time-consuming work and there is no one there that will push you along. Don't start unless you are really committed to doing what it takes to get the business going and can motivate yourself to grow the business.

You must also be financially prepared for the business you are going to start. You probably will not be able to draw much money from the business for a while. This may be a few months if you have no fixed costs. If you buy a lot of equipment or real estate, you may not be able to draw out much money for a longer period after paying for your loans. Can you live without the paycheck?

You should also be able to shoulder the risk you are taking on. Many businesses fail, some by lack of hard or smart work and some due to no reason of the owner's efforts. What will happen to your limited retirement nest egg if this happens? Can you financially live with a failure if that happens?

Do you have the business skills that you need to run the business? Many of us worked in performing a limited task in a large company and have little experience in accounts receivable, collections, accounts payable juggling, inventory control and the like. Do you really have the experience to run the entire business? Are you prepared to make the necessary decisions in a timely manner as is required in many businesses?

Since we are talking about retirement age people starting a business, you should look at your physical well-being and stamina to truthfully analyze if you are physically capable. Think of the lugging and lifting that would be necessary to own one of those festival sales businesses. Is that what you are capable of doing each weekend?

Somewhere along the way, you will have to be a good salesman. You will either have to sell to your ultimate customers or you will have to convince a retailer to sell your product. Don't believe if you have a good product that the customers will beat a path to your door. Nice thought but that rarely happens. Are you a good salesperson? Maybe you should take a course at a community college before you think about starting your business.

Those required skills

I mentioned that you need a lot of basic skills. I remember at my first place of employment, I had contact with departments that handled accounts receivable, accounts payable, customer service representatives, accounting, legal issues, inventory control personnel, sale, marketing and shipping/receiving. I didn't have to understand how to do those functions. But in small businesses, these functions are all rolled into your position as the owner.

You must have some level of knowledge of accounting. But with easy to use software, you can learn enough about accounting in a 4-hour training session on the software to enter everything into the database and review your weekly or monthly results, to make sure you are on track with your expectations.

Selling and marketing is a critical part of many of these businesses. You must have some skills in this area so you can write advertisements and articles about your business and put together signage for your location. A lot of these businesses rely on taste and smell to attract customers followed by a selling discussion with you, the on-location sale's person. Many of the opportunities listed identify specific advertising venues to use.

Customer service is critical in these small businesses and is an attitude that you the owner must have. If customers wanted poor customer service, they can go to the big discount stores and get poor customer service at half the price. You should know how to treat customers so they will come back and they will refer you to their friends.

Inventory control is one of the skills that has doomed many small businesses. Too much inventory and you have too much money tied up in the business to ever show a profit. Too little inventory and you will run out of the high selling items, leaving half the potential customers that you attract to leave empty handed. There are computer programs that can help with inventory management if it is a significant part of your business.

Manufacturing may apply to your business. You should know every step of the operation even if you are having others do it for you. If things go wrong you need to know how to solve the problems.

Go through everything that will be required to operate your business and make sure you know or learn how to handle these functions.

Franchises

I frequently get asked about franchises since the OLD conventional wisdom is that they have a much higher rate of success. I highlight the OLD in conventional wisdom because in more recent studies they have shown that <u>now</u> franchises have higher rates of failure than independent startup businesses. In certain business categories, franchises have a much higher failure rate. They may work best for you but for most people buying a franchise it is not the way to go. Most are meant for full time businesses where you are willing to risk a lot of money.

Many of the big name franchises are obviously not the subject of this book since they cost hundreds of thousands of dollars up to millions of dollars to start. But there are a number of small franchises where you sell a product in your neighborhood or repair a specific item, working out of your home and using mail services to deliver the product to the client. These may make a good business for you. But some make a good business for the franchise and leave little profit for you.

I tell everyone who is seriously thinking about getting into a franchise to have a specialized franchise lawyer read over the offering circular. They know what to look for in those offerings and they know what works and what doesn't. Most people who haven't been through the franchising process many times won't be able to find the one or two killer sentences in a document that goes on for hundreds of pages. I also recommend people apply for a Small Business Administration (SBA) backed loan for their franchise business. You may not need the loan but the SBA is great at tracking which franchises succeed and which don't. They know which franchises have unreasonable terms in their offering and which meet the standard conditions. The SBA compiles a "no-no" list of franchises that they will not lend money to buy. The SBA lenders will turn down your loan request quickly and tell you that the SBA won't underwrite the loan for that franchise. So even if you don't end up taking a loan, if your SBA approved lender says no to you on a loan, there may be good justification.

Everyone loves their franchise when they are learning the business. Everyone should love their franchise if the name brand brings customers to their door. But after the learning period is done and the business is running well, unless the name brand recognition is the key to your success, most people hate to pay the ongoing franchise fees or the high markups on the products they need to buy. But you have to continue paying the royalties and you are frequently restrained from starting a similar independent business on your own.

Certain types of businesses have books published on how to start them. You can look at any of the entrepreneur magazines and find a large advertisement on how to start many types of business. In the few that I have looked at, I think you will learn over 80% of what a franchise will teach you. These books will also provide wholesale contacts and other critical information that will take you months to learn on your own. Take a look at www.smallbizbooks.com for an example. For the $70 or $80 charge for these books, they could be a great value to you and save you a lot of time and mistakes. You could also simply get a job in your target industry and learn the business from a successful operation and then go on and start your own business.

MLM Multilevel Marketing or Network Marketing

I think most people have heard of this way of marketing products. One sales person works for another member who works for many more members up the line. It may seem like the product price is highly marked up compared to manufacturing costs. Every member on the organization chart above the person actually selling the product is collecting payments on their sales. But compared to the overhead of year-around storefronts, on-going operating costs and distributor mark ups that a retailer has to build into his product price, you may find retailers' pricing similar to a good MLM organization. A few of the early MLM companies have given the industry a bad reputation. Some are good but I still believe most people who get involved wish they hadn't.

It's no secret that the most money is made by people who find candidates to join the organization under them, hence collecting some of the profit from all of their sales and all of the sales that their new candidates make and the sales tiers down the organization. Building up a large organization is the key to success in MLM, not necessarily selling a normal amount of product yourself.

You may also run into minimum monthly purchases from many of these programs. When sales go down, you continue buying at the minimum amount. If sales come back, all is well; you sell off the excess product that you have been buying over the slow sales months. If the product has gone out of vogue, many people are stuck with vast amounts of unsaleable inventory in their basement and see much of their profits over the proceeding months, eaten up by the ongoing mandatory inventory purchases. But a lot of excess inventory can be avoided if you are allowed to have an "end of the season" sale to unload this inventory even if it is at cost or at a slight loss. Like all other businesses, you must manage your inventory. The MLM organization just cares that you continue to buy the products from them.

If a MLM organization is your desire, you will probably be contacted by hundreds of groups if you let the word get out that you are looking for a MLM position. I will not cover much more on this type of business.

I want you to realize that MLM is not the only type of home-based network sales businesses. Many suppliers will allow you to sell their products from your home inventory or even drop ship their products directly to your customers. There are a lot of Internet sales businesses that provide retail sales.

Financing your business

I ask you not to consider starting a business that is going to require you to borrow a lot of money, compared to your retirement nest egg. This book is focused on small businesses that require little money to start. The more you borrow, the more you risk. If you decide to borrow, think of these avenues to look into.

Borrowing money from your retirement account Look carefully into the consequences that this borrowing will have on your compound earnings, the tax implications, and what this will mean if your business fails and you don't have the cash to repay your loan. This option may have the lowest interest rate.

Borrowing from a bank using a commercial loan This will normally require that you personally guarantee the loan or put up some collateral. Know what you will loose if you don't pay it back.

Borrowing from an SBA backed bank This normally takes a much longer time for approval and closing than a regular bank loan. You will have to provide a mortgage on your house, personally guarantee it and possibly provide some additional collateral. You will need a short business plan. The interest rates are normally 2.5% above the prime rate.

Buying your startup needs on a credit card This is probably the least favorable of the options since the interest rates are higher here than on bank loans. This option will require no approval and can be completed immediately.

Equipment loans This can be a good option if your basic startup investment is in equipment. Frequently, equipment sales organizations have special or subsidized interest rates to sell more equipment.

If equipment is the big cost, consider leasing the equipment. You will still be required to pay off the entire lease so you are not reducing your risk, but at least this minimizes the startup capital required.

Special development grants and loans Investigate if these are available for you and your business. These are more available for protected classes of people or starting businesses in poor economic areas. Always look into these special loans by talking with economic development people in the county and city where you are starting your business.

But remember that you will always be required to pay back any loan short of filing for bankruptcy. So decide how much you can afford to lose.

Working Capital

Besides a bad business model, the factor that causes the most business failures is too little working capital. Always plan on needing a lot more money than anticipated to do all of the things needed to get the business going.

Make sure you have enough money to adequately stock your shelves. Shelves with one product in front and nothing behind is often a turn off to customers.

Make sure that you can pay all of your bills and all of your employees for 3 to 6 months if sufficient business does not walk into your establishment.

Make sure that you have allotted enough money to do adequate advertising. Figuring out what is adequate is the biggest business plan mistake that I see people make.

Make sure that your financial plan assumes that you will not get any payment before it is due. If you give your customers 30,60 or 90 days to pay, none will pay before the last day. And you will be chasing many of them for your money long after it is due.

Make sure you know where you will come up with extra cash if everything takes much longer than anticipated to be completed.

Traits to look for in your business

There are certain traits to look for in a business to increase your chances of success.

Low initial cost for you If you can buy everything you need to get going for a few thousand dollars, you only risk losing the value of your initial investment and a lot of hours of your time. This is a very good investment and the risk that you take is limited to the size of your investment. You can minimize the risk even more if you have some equipment that you have been using for your hobby and use that equipment to start your business. You have very little investment in startup costs and are mainly risking your time to start the business. Competition may have to spend more money to get into the business than you had to spend. If you run across a grouping of used equipment available at a real discount that is needed to run such a business, you might have a significant advantage over any potential competition.

Low fixed cost If you need to sign a multi-year lease for space or equipment to run your business, you will be taking a big risk. Most times the leasing agent will make you personally guarantee the lease so you are going to pay for the lease even if your company goes broke. Long-term leases are not for retired people. You have an ongoing monthly cost for your business without a guarantee of monthly revenue. These types of businesses are high risk. But if you are working from home, a trailer or your back yard and own any equipment outright if you do not make any money in a specific month, you shouldn't incur any costs except your time.

Look for a business that is not dependent on marketing and advertisement. A lot of companies spend over 50% of their revenue on advertising. That may be a good idea for them, and with large sales volumes, it could pay off. Bigger companies have a definite advantage over your small business. Look for products that people must see, smell or taste as the main mechanism to market the product.

There are a lot of businesses with historically few customers and you wonder how the owner makes a living. Maybe that's just what you want, a product that can be a nice supplemental business but can't make a full-time living. Think if there is a way to sell that product without the high fixed cost that an unsuccessful owner has to absorb.

Some of these businesses may be seasonal businesses, making lots of money for 3 months a year but risk losing money the other 9 months paying the rent. Is there someone else out there who could use and rent the facility during your off season? Everyone sees the ski retailers that now have integrated patio furniture during the summer. The ice cream stands now turn into Christmas tree stands during the winter. Or the Christmas gift stores that will try to put in anything else during the summer. Maybe you can have a trailer or mobile stand to run your business from and just rent some land to set it on during your season. Can you rent a kiosk at the local mall for a few months?

Other benefits

There are added benefits to owning your own business. The business may bring some benefit by offsetting some of your personal costs or some of your tax burden. I'm no expert in accounting so ask your accountant how these might impact your personal tax burden and wealth.

Utilizing your basement or your back yard to conduct your business.

Traveling to your hobby conventions that have now turned into a required function of your hobby business.

Owning the property where your business is located and renting it to the business, allowing some of the cash flow of your business to be claimed as passive rental income and not as personal income.

Using your car, your phone or a portion of your home utilities for your business.

Making sure you understand how any profits might impact your social security and other pension plans.

Providing a lifestyle that will allow you to travel to festivals and move around selling your product and is this of value to you.

Being free to follow your dream, work on a schedule that fits your life, not having a boss and having autonomy in your life may all be your desires.

Exit Strategy

You should always have an exit strategy in place.

You may not be making money and have to financially close shop. How much can you realistically sell your inventory and machinery for to get out of the business? You may be able to find the value of your equipment's vintage on-line. This will help you realistically determine how big a financial risk you are taking from the start.

But what if you get sick for a short period. Can your spouse or a good friend take over the business? Can you just let it go idle for a few months? It may be a lot easier for your back up person if you keep a very specific procedure book with exacting details on how every step of every operation is completed.

What happens if you are doing well and you suddenly become incapacitated? Can you think of a way to keep the business going without your physical activity involved, just your thinking and directions? If you come up with a resolution to this problem, make sure you write it down so your spouse/partner will know exactly what you expect them to do in the short term.

Is your business sellable to others? You might want to sit down with a business broker and discuss the possibilities of selling your business. If it is a small business, go to the Sunbelt Business Broker's web site at www.Sunbeltnetwork.com or if it has grown to a substantial size, go to International Mergers & Acquisitions web site at www.IMA-world.com. Find an intermediary or business broker who can work with you and provide an idea of what your business is currently worth and what factors are used to determine the value. You may want to be prepared for your estate executor to sign an agreement with one of these agents if you should suddenly need to get out.

Many businesses that are based on your skills or that show little profit above your paycheck may not have sufficient value to cover the cost of the broker's expenses. You may be able to sell off the equipment quickly to an equipment broker and get rid of the inventory through a going-out-of-business sale. This may be your best option. But make sure you investigate these possibilities before you are in need and leave specific instructions and contacts to make if someone else has to handle the arrangements.

Business Reference Material

I mentioned earlier in the book the company that runs the web site www.smallbizbooks.com. I have seen a few of their manuals. They cover a number of businesses I mention in the idea sections, such as auto detailing, consulting, self-publishing, cleaning services, senior care, selling crafts, event planning, gift baskets, personal concierge, specialty travel, and bed and breakfasts. They also have books on some general business topics, such as selling your products, writing a business plan, starting a business, and specific guidance on a state-by-state basis for start up requirements in specific states

If you go on any of the large bookstore sites, you will find hundreds of books covering startup of many types of businesses and general business start-up guidance.

The Small Business Administration has a large on-line library of helpful pamphlets and forms that you might need available free or inexpensively at www.SBA.gov. Go to the library section. There are hundreds of books. Some give specific information on how to write a business plan on specific types of business. Others talk about inventory management and doing market research. One booklet you must read is MP-12 Checklist for Going Into Business. Also look for Small Business Basics from SCORE and see their web site www.score.org .

The IRS offers a start-up business kit that you can request through their web site.

Opening a home-based garden and tree growing business sounds quite easy if you look at www.freeplants.com. He sells a kit that teaches you all you need to know to run this business in your 1/6-acre back yard.

Go to the business section of any library and you will find numerous books on start-up actions that you must take. Talk to other small business people in the industry you want to enter. Find a networking organization of small business people to talk with about their efforts.

If after reading through my list of possible business, you still haven't found something that you like, go try the magazine section of a large bookstore. There are many magazines with entrepreneur, franchise, business opportunity, and start-up in their title that will provide thousands of additional ideas. Some may only be appropriate for full time businesses or ones that require large start up money commitments. But there are others that may fill your needs. There are a number of franchises and distributorships that are identified in the classified sections of these books.

Due Diligence

Before you start any business or buy an existing business, you need to do an in-depth review of the facts and your plans. This is called due diligence. For some of these small businesses, the need to do this may be very limited.

I always recommend that you see an accountant or tax preparer to make sure you know the tax implications of starting the business. Will income from this business impact any retirement plan monies you are now collecting? Will the business expenses change what you are paying in taxes? Some of these professionals will have a brief chat with you and provide some information on a free or inexpensive initial consult. Others will have the time clock running from the moment you hit the waiting room. So know in advance what you will pay for their services.

The next thing that you may need professional help from a lawyer or accountant is how to organize your business. Should you be a sole proprietor, an S section business, and LLC or a C section business? There are hundreds of factors that will feed into this selection including the liability risk of the type of business you are starting.

Many of the businesses we talk about can be started on a shoestring. Baking some pies in your home oven and selling them at a local fair might cost you $100 in materials and a few hours of your time. Taking some of your hobby output and selling it may have similar low initial costs. Don't over-analyze these types of businesses. Try it and see what the response is. Don't spend weeks trying to figure out if your product will sell. Try it.

Other businesses will cost more to start and you should take the time to look into it more. Go to someone who is operating a similar business, maybe in another area of town or in another city (you can possibly find them through an Internet search) and strike up a conversation with these people. Ask them for recommendations of things to do and things not to do. If they don't see you as a direct competitor due to differences in your product lines or your geographic location, they may be willing to help you. Go to your SCORE (Senior Core of Retired Executives) office at the SBA and ask for assistance from someone with the expertise you need.

Take your product and try to sell it at a festival or other location. This may not be how you plan on selling your product in your business plan but you may get good feedback from some potential customers on what they really think about your product and how much they would realistically pay for your product.

Look for suppliers and professional organizations to provide helpful start up recommendations. Put together a business plan. Go into a friendly banker to apply for a loan. They normally give you a lot of feedback on what type of problems they see with your type of business. Have friends and people already in the business read your business plan and provide you feedback.

Look over the financial section of your business plan and really make sure all of the expenses you will have in your business are included. Misjudging startup costs is one of the big mistakes a start up business can make. There are a lot of incidental costs that they forget to include. Do an honest appraisal of how much time you will have to put in the business for the first year. Make sure the profits are in line with what you need to earn to invest the time that it will take. I frequently tell people to double the first guess of the hours they will need to put in for a more accurate guess as to the hours it will really take to get going.

If you know a few potential customers personally, go to them and ask them for their opinions on your product. Take samples so you can get them to take a good look. Some business people will help you do this even if they do not know you. Just catch them at a time when they can spare a few minutes.

A few warnings

A lot of small businesses neglect to adequately check into all of the legal matters. Many problems can arise from ignoring these requirements. I recommend that you look into the following matters carefully. You may get advice from others in the business that you are entering that they have never gotten caught not following these restrictions. The risks and penalties could become excessive if you violate the legal requirements.

Licenses
Many businesses require licenses to operate. Just once have I seen a lemonade stand operator get caught. I've never heard of a small farmer's stand getting in trouble. Cooking goods or selling items for human consumption usually have manufacturing restrictions such as a certified kitchen and special health permits.

Zoning
Many uses of your home or your property may not be allowed especially if it is zoned residential. Check into whether your business can operate on your premises. Many people may operate their business for years in violation of the zoning, but the bigger and more profitable your business gets, the more chance that you will get questioned.

Sales Tax
Many tabletop retail operations at flea markets, farm markets and festivals don't charge sales tax. But you may have a big tax bill if you ever get questioned. Many of these operations will require that you have a sales tax number just to set up your table.

IRS and your Revenues

Many people operating small cash businesses don't report their earnings to the IRS. Again, this may be very common but it could be a big burden if you finally get questioned on it.

Insurance

Your home and car insurance may stipulate that your coverage only covers non-commercial use. You don't want to check what this means after an extensive automobile accident. Or you don't want to find out when someone coming to your residence for business slips on your sidewalk. Look into proper coverage for your business.

Mini-Business Plan

Executive Summary takes one sentence to summarize every 1 or 2 paragraphs in the plan. Skip this if your plan is under 5 pages.

Describe your business product in detail.

Describe how you will organize your business and who will be doing every step of the business.

Describe the market you are in and discuss competition and make sure you talk about your sustainable competitive advantage.

Talk about how you will finance the start-up costs of your business and describe, in general, the equipment and leases you will be taking on.

Put together a one to three year budget for your business on an item-by-item basis so a reader can see if you are missing any obvious costs that you will incur.

Put together what you will charge for your product(s) including some justification of how you got to that price and how it compares to the competition. Don't guess on the competition's pricing. Check it out.

Put together a sales target for your business and provide some justification to show these levels aren't just guesses or wishful thinking.

Put together a profit statement based on your sales, pricing and costs.

Put together a statement on how you will know if you should exit the business through closing down or selling out.

Business Opportunity Listings

The following portion of this book contains a number of suggestions of businesses that you can start to provide extra income. Some of these businesses are really lifestyle businesses that will not bring in a lot of income for most people but will allow you to expense against your business revenue a number of activities that you may be paying for out of your pocket. This may add a lot of enjoyment to your life.

Some of these businesses rely on already owning an excess asset, such as free use of a large basement area in your house or having hundreds of acres of land that you do not want to sell and can put that land to use to generate some income.

Some of the businesses have specific marketing ideas that you can follow that will limit the size of your business but may provide a competitive advantage by your focus.

Some of these businesses are totally new in concept as a profit making commercial business. Some of these may be a more common business but the book proposes a change to the common commercial model to allow you to have a smaller business with a lot less fixed costs. These changes are identified.

I have also stated a subjective estimate on how expensive these businesses will be to start up using the proposed model. The ones that have high startup costs probably should not be considered unless you already own the expensive assets that you will need to operate the business. Many of these involve owning real estate. Some involve owning equipment for a hobby business. You may be able to try out the business using your lighter duty hobby equipment to test the market before upgrading to expensive commercial equipment that will last longer.

I have identified which areas I have seen franchises operate in. Always check out these websites and franchises to learn more about the business even if you don't want to consider a franchise. You can usually do a web search on the subject using any of the search engines.

Additional information on many of these listings can be found on the web site www.StanSpector.com

Advocate

Type: Part time
Startup costs: Minimal
Location: Home based

There are a number of government benefit systems that are difficult for people to navigate. Applying for various government benefits such as Medicaid, Medicare, Social Security Disability and Disability Insurance coverage is an arduous task. This process is too difficult for disabled, sick and elderly people. There are large companies and various law firms that will help you through the process and charge a very large fee to do it. While these systems may be difficult to navigate, in most cases, it is not difficult enough to warrant these large fees.

Starting up a simple business to help people through these systems can be rewarding. You must learn the rules of the system and follow them exactly. Numerous service agencies provide training for volunteer advocates. This may be the best way to start out in this sector. After you have built up experience, you can start charging reasonable hourly fees to help your clients. Use senior and disabled publications to advertise your business.

There are also advocates, frequently volunteers, who advocate in hospitals for patients to make sure they are getting the care they need. Contact the elderly's children to hire you to make frequent checkups and advocate for their parents. Become a member of the National Association of Professional Geriatric Care Managers (GCM) so you can earn the $80 to $200 per hour they charge.

After-school activities for students

Type: Part time during the school year
Startup costs: Low
Location: Rented

Many working parents don't want their children at home alone after school every day. Run a camp or some training program where you provide some specific activity for the children. You are providing an activity while watching the children for the working parents. Athletics, art, acting, and computer training are just a few of the areas you may be successful in developing this business. Don't get into the day care venue unless you want to be involved with a lot of regulation.

You must rent a facility in the right location. Locate in areas where the school bus system will drop the children off right in front of your business so the parents are free from making drop off arrangements themselves. Advertising for this business will be necessary and word-of-mouth may follow if you are successful. There are some music, exercise and learning based franchises that you can investigate to see what type of activities others are doing.

Your business may offer something different to do for children's birthday parties on the weekends. Try outfitting a bus with children's activities and taking that around to school yards for after school gym activities or art activities and take it to homes for birthday parties.

Antique Dealer/Restoring

Type: Part time/hobby
Startup costs: Medium/low
Location: Rented

One of the all-time hobby business favorites is opening an antique store. You may have built up an expertise in a certain period or style of antiques as a hobby. You will have built up additional expertise in a very wide array of antiques to serve a wider market to sustain a business. Pick up inventory through shrewd garage sale purchases, estate sales or auctions. Many avid collectors may have an overabundance of startup inventory that they already own.

You should consider renting a stall at a cooperative for a few months before jumping into a full store. Marketing is done through media advertisements for your own shop. If you belong to a cooperative, you will have much lower advertising costs since joint advertising is often used or is paid for through your rent. Certain neighborhoods and locations are known for their antique shops so locating in these areas would minimize any advertising costs.

Your interest may be more in the line of refinishing antiques. You may want to start in refinishing by working with a few antique shops refinishing items for them. This activity is not suitable for working on down your basement due to the chemicals used but a detached garage or barn may work out fine. For a refinishing business, leave a card or brochure in a number of antique shops and share a referral fee with the shop owner for business they refer to you. This type of business can be started up at a low cost.

Auto detailing and doll up

Type: Part time
Startup costs: Low
Location: Customer's site or rented

If car work is enjoyable to you, this may be a business opportunity that you can get into with a minimum of equipment. Do these services at the customer's home or work location so you don't compete against the big car cleaning franchises. Check out the fixed location franchises' prices and services to keep competitive. There are also franchises that target parking areas.

Advertise in local media or pass out circulars in a target neighborhood. If you plan on offering the service during working hours in large companys' parking lots, put circulars on windshields of the cars while people are working.

Bar-B-Q caterer

Type: Part time
Startup costs: Medium/high
Location: Home office

This requires some type of cooking setup that you tow behind your vehicle. You go to parties at homes, businesses or park pavilions and provide some traditional grilling or smoking of the meal. This can be as simple as hotdogs, hamburgers, veggie burgers and portabella mushrooms cooked over a grill and served with various salads for graduation and birthday parties in people's back yard on the weekends. These types of rolling cookers are moderately priced. Many equipment suppliers can be found on the Internet that will also help you get your business going.

There are dozens of companies selling full smoker setups that can be towed. This will allow you to slow cook a full line of meats for higher priced fare. There are recipes and equipment for cooking meat and side dishes all over the Internet. However, these full service set-ups can get quite expensive since many are full service kitchens.

Market using local media advertising and posters in the area. Make sure to have your card and a menu at every event you cater so you can network your name around to the guests. If you see someone that has the right crowd coming to their event, provide a discount to make sure you get that job.

This will require licensing in most areas to provide this prepared food service.

Bartending

Type: Part time
Startup costs: Minimal
Location: At the clients location

Tend bar at people's homes or corporate facilities for those private events. Work for caterers providing the service for them. Normally, you will not need a liquor license if you are pouring the drinks provided by the host but check into regulations and liability closely.

Pass your card around and advertise in select media. Have your card at all events to get your name spread. There are franchises in this area but I can't figure out why you would join one. Check state laws about your liability in the event of a patron's accident.

Bed and Breakfast

Type: Lifestyle/seasonal
Startup costs: High
Location: Fixed, owned location

Opening a B&B can be a big job. It is always an expensive task. Getting known and filling your rooms can be an even bigger task. Costs are high for the building and bringing that building up to code requirements for rental rooms. But many people who get one going find it is a wonderful lifestyle. Look for a location with high interest activities nearby that people will want to come to visit. Putting a B&B in a location just because you own the building is not usually successful.

There are a number of books, magazines, local tourist brochures and web sites that focus all or part of the publication on bed and breakfast locations that you will need to advertise in. Get on the chamber of commerce list for housing in your area. Put brochures in other tourist attractions if you are near some. Offer to put their brochures in your lobby

Depending on your location, room use may be very seasonal.

Bring in extra income by making tour arrangements for clients or allowing private chefs to prepare meals for top paying customers in your kitchen and dining room.

Brokering

Type: Part time/full time
Startup costs: Low
Location: Home based

There are brokers out there who are acting as middlemen for almost any product. We are all familiar with real estate brokers and loan brokers but have you thought about selling small businesses? There are a few franchises brokering businesses.

You can also broker materials such as paper (for printers), guns, tools and equipment, specialty chemicals, yachts, specialty foods, new cars, used cars, trucking and freight, air charters, event tickets, franchises and metals. You can try almost any supplies used by manufacturing where buyers spend a lot of time searching and bidding out for the lowest price. The company's owner does not have the time to spend doing a thorough job.

There are people who broker subcontract work for manufacturing companies. If you have some machining to do, you can either send it to a few companies in the area that you know about or hire a broker to solicit a large number of quotes. The broker can find more companies out of the area and knows the strengths and weaknesses of each. The broker spends a lot more time bidding out this work than the infrequent times when an owner does it. This can also come in very handy for the owner when he has a rush job. The broker should know who is busy and who isn't. He may also prevail on a shop to do the work quickly if he is a frequent customer there where the owner will not have that clout.

There are also international manufacturing brokers. You may be buying or even making a product. Give this product to one of these brokers and they can source it to China, India or a host of other countries depending on the product. Many people find they can have it produced and shipped back to their location a lot cheaper than they can manufacture it.

There are used book brokers who buy books from school districts who will discontinue using a certain book and resell it to another district who will start using it. You can broker just about anything.

Business center for a captive audience

Type: Full time/part time
Startup costs: High
Location: A site with a large enough captive audience

Airports and hotels all over the country are installing business centers. These businesses provide equipment that the business people may not be able to carry with them. Most of the prime locations are taken and probably pay a lot of rent or are run by the location as a profit center. A full service business center can involve a lot of expensive equipment.

Contact smaller hotels and rental apartments to find a good niche for you to serve. Don't compete against the big office supply houses for the high volume services they provide. Provide the services and equipment to use at the location where these people are.

Advertise using signs for the captive audience and skip media advertising.

Caravan guide

Type: Lifestyle/seasonal
Startup costs: low
Location: Home based

If you are into RV'ing, become a historical expert on a trail that you can take other RV'ers touring. Things like Route 66, Route 1, the Oregon or Santa Fe trails, Lewis and Clark's tour, women's suffrage trail, and hundreds of other historic paths are things that you can become expert or use your knowledge as the tour guide. If you don't already have an RV, you are probably not the right person for this culture. Look to the RV publications for your advertising. Giving financial credits for customers who refer others to you may help get the word spread about your business.

On-board communications systems for each customer might be a nice touch. This will allow you to provide your lecture information while everyone is driving between locations.

If you don't like RV'ing, maybe you can set up similar historical bus tours using local hotels along the way.

Card maker

Type: Hobby
Startup costs: Low
Location: Home based

You notice when you get a card or an invitation that is printed on hand-made paper. They stand out from all of the store-bought cards. If some company can manufacture a similar product in large quantities, then you just haven't found a good niche.

But if you love making paper with different materials and colors mixed up in the pulp, you have a product that people will buy. They probably are all somewhat unique but you make up batches of the pulp, maybe even in your blender, and turn it into a card. You might find people who want a dozen or two for their own use that will have a distinctive color or style that you reserve for them. You may find someone who wants a unique invitation and will pay the money for your work. Some companies may want their holiday cards to stand out and will commission larger batches.

Advertise in small business publications. Contact mid-sized companies directly and send a sample to the top executives. Have traditional card shops retail your product for you offering half the ultimate price for their sales effort. Some on-line sales may be possible through your own web site or some distributor's site.

Also, think about making small hand-cast paper boxes. These sell well at local gift shops and festivals. You can use other hand-made techniques for your cards but they must be significantly different from the commercial products.

Cash/Coin Operated Businesses

Type: Part time
Startup costs: High
Location: Fixed

People love coin-operated businesses. They love the idea of dropping by every evening to pick up their paycheck in cash and reporting what they feel like to the IRS. Well, things aren't that simple.

Laundromats and car wash facilities dominate this sector. There are a lot of franchises and suppliers that brand their equipment name so you might appear like a franchise to some customers. Both of these have fairly high building costs. They also each require some work daily to keep the equipment clean and filled with necessary supplies to operate. But both do make a good business and you may find someone who is looking for an hour or two of work a day that will restock and clean up the place.

Another sector in this area is game rooms. Large companies already take many of the prime locations. Most of the large locations will mandate that someone be there during the long hours they are open. They all require frequent update of the equipment to the newest rage in games. This sector has high startup costs and long hours. Even though it can provide a large cash flow, it is not appropriate for most readers of this book since it is a much larger scale operation involving many employees. You may be able to convince a bar, restaurant or laundromat owner to allow you to put a few machines in their operations and share with them half of your revenue. This is a good way to start out as a small operation without a lot of financial risk.

Catering and private chef

Type: Part time
Startup costs: Low
Location: Home based

Start by cooking some meals in people's homes for a dinner party as their personal chef. Use the dishes and kitchen in the house you are working in so you have a minimal investment. This normally requires no licensing. There are franchises for private chefs but I don't know why.

If this is successful, move on up to doing small catering jobs renting trucks, place settings, serving utensils, tables and bars. Try these steps before getting too involved in the full service catering business where you supply all of the equipment. At this point, you may be required to have food safety training and require licensing in some locations. Advertise in local media and pass out cards at every event.

Be a traditional caterer and take on as many or as few jobs as you want. Give a recommended specialty menu for your clients before trying to prepare whatever the host wants.

Don't want to really be a cook? Well, try something simple where you can become expert. The chocolate fountains are used for desserts at many parties. Rent out your service for cutting up fruit, cakes, cookies and other items to dip into the chocolate fountain. Rent the fountain and sell the chocolate mix. Some hotels and some hostesses may want the table manned during the prime time of use.

Christmas decorator

Type: Seasonal
Startup costs: Low/medium
Location: Home office

Own lawn decorations and set them up on customers' lawns for Christmas or other holidays. Charge for rent of the decorations and the set up time. Provide set up of owner's lighting decorations. Now more people will consider this in their busy lives.

Believe it or not, there are franchises in this field. Check them out to see their offerings. For advertising, try passing door-to-door handouts in a limited neighborhood. You might try some local newspaper advertising also.

Always make up a plan or drawing that your customer agrees to in writing before you start and make sure that you produce what you agreed to produce.

This can be dangerous work if you are in a northern climate and working on snowy surfaces.

Coaching

Type: Part time
Startup costs: Low
Location: At your client's location

You can be a personal, life or business coach for other people. If you have good business skills, you can be a big help to business owners since it is sometimes easier for an outsider to see the problems and solutions. Frequently, the business owners have made decisions that started the problem and are not unbiased as to the cause or resolution. You can objectively look at what is going on. There may be a number of ideas a business owner might want to bounce off an expert. But they are afraid to get an active industry consultant involved unless they have a confidentiality agreement with someone who is not likely to talk with their competitors. Depending on your experience level, this can be a lucrative business. Marketing for this is mostly referrals from past clients and your personal network.

You might have been through personal hard times, such as certain medical conditions, that will allow you to coach others going through the same situation. Make sure that you stay out of diagnosis and treatment and stay on more philosophical coaching.

You can just be a general coach for people's day-to-day concerns and life problems or how they can get their professional work going better.

Coffee Carts

Type: Part time
Startup costs: Low to Medium
Location: Find the right high traffic location or move around to where the people are for short periods of time.

This is different from opening a full-blown coffee shop that requires high fixed costs for rent in a retail location, ongoing employee problems, and high utilities. Look into setting up a small, mobile cart or kiosk that you can operate. Try a business office
in the morning or a busy nightlife location in the evening. Keep the hours short, the menu simple and find a good location to work. There are franchises in this sector so check out what they are doing. Licensing may be required depending on what you are serving.

College bound student's services

Type: Seasonal
Startup costs: Low
Location: At the clients' premises

People are making a good business helping college bound students get into the college of their choice. Consulting in testing preparation, college selection, essay writing, and application completion are critical for getting into the college of their choice. There are franchises in certain areas of this sector. This is a lot of work to learn all of that you need to do to succeed for the students. High schools offer courses for the students that you may attend as a parent. Many books are published on the subject.

Advertise in student publications or PTA brochures. You will get businesses through referrals from satisfied customers.

College campus publication

Type: Part time
Startup costs: Low
Location: Home office

Put together a publication for a nearby college neighborhood. Plenty of businesses serving this clientele will advertise in a publication if it has a good circulation. Have plenty of coupons for cheap food. Have articles about what's going on for nightlife and on-campus activities. There are some franchises in this business but they are rare. Focus on the students and campus to be successful.

The basic model for this business is passing out the paper free. You have to get businesses to pay for advertising. Try a low introductory advertising price for the first one or two issues and have the customer place a coupon in your publication. They will know quickly if advertising with you has brought them customers.

Concierge

Type: Part time
Startup costs: Low
Location: Home office or business lobby

Provide services such as errands, dry cleaning, laundry drop off, event tickets and reservations for busy people. Look for a company that will let you set up in their lobby during shift start and end to provide the services for their employees. Try tennis and exercise club lobbies or independent care facilities for this type of business. There are franchises in this sector so check out what they offer. Have a brochure and your business cards to hand out to potential patrons. Advertise in the facility's newsletter.

Offer similar services to people at home. They will call you up and provide the instructions for what they want. They may give you the key to their garage or house for the services. Advertising in local media will be necessary if you operate by phone from your home.

Concrete coatings

Type: Part time-seasonal
Startup costs: Medium to high
Location: Home based

Many damaged surfaces can be improved with the modern coatings that you can apply in a number of colors, textures and designs. Swimming pool decks, garages, driveways and sidewalks are a few of the surfaces that you can improve. Have a nice book put together of past jobs that you have completed and allow potential customers to call your happy customers for references.

Do a search on-line to see the diversity of what is offered by competing suppliers.

There are a number of suppliers that will provide you training and help in starting a business without any ongoing charges beyond committing to buy materials from them. This may be as good as some of the franchises in the sector. Hire someone to do the labor and you do the selling and bidding. You might be able to start with $10,000 in inventory plus a truck. The money buys you a sufficient material supply to do a number of jobs and some of the basic equipment. You might spend up to $50,000 to start a franchise that requires more equipment.

Don't limit yourself to floors only. Similar materials provide unique finishes to indoor and outdoor walls that do not paint well.

Advertise in the local media and focus on special issues that cover summer and swimming pool activities. Pass out circulars door-to-door to houses that are in need of your business.

Consulting

Type: Part time to full time
Startup costs: Low
Location: Home based

If you have an area of expertise, you may be able to sell your expertise to companies in need. Think about contacting companies that cannot afford a full time person to do the service that you provide. Maybe larger companies have peak load times which they need extra help and you should make them aware of your availability during the busy season. Develop a special program, pattern, or methodology so you can explain to the potential client how you do business and how this method will help their company. Usually, if you cannot show a company more profits than your service will cost them, they will not hire you. So put the time in before any sales calls to put together material that will show how you will help them achieve a positive cash flow improvement if they hire you. All marketing for how you will help them achieve this type of business is personal contacts and initial presentation.

Contractor referral service

Type: Part time
Startup costs: Low
Location: Home based

People are always looking for reputable contractors to do work around their home or business. You can be the conduit for putting together successful matches. It may be hard to make money from just giving out the name of a contractor who does a specific type of work. Building material companies usually have posting boards at their entrances for posting business card from contractors.

You can charge a fee to contractors for finding them work to bid on, if they eventually get the contract for this work. This will be added on to the existing work they find on their own. They normally have to spend a lot on advertising to get their customers.

Know your referral contractors well. Know how they will compete price-wise and quality wise. Know their honesty record and their current availability and know all of the contractors' specialties. You can provide a great service.

If you get involved in monitoring the work, the customers may agree to pay a fee. You might consider bonding contactors, acting as a middle man for progress payments, making recommendations for the contracts for the work or even checking out and approving critical steps that happen when the customer is not available.

Coupon books

Type: Part time/full time
Startup costs: Low
Location: Home based

Each major city has coupon books covering restaurants and entertainment venues. Why not another one with a little different focus? Try your book with a neighborhood focus or a resort town that is too small to have it's own major book. You could try to have discount coupons on clothing and grocery stores instead of having restaurants and entertainment only. Check out what the franchises in this sector are offering.

The businesses offering coupons pay you a fee for putting their coupon in your book. The more copies you distribute, the more they will pay you. So you will have to have a way of tracking how many you print and how many are actually bought. You might also put a special code on the coupons so the advertisers will be able to track how many customers come in and use your booklet.

This business requires door-to-door marketing to get the businesses to put coupons in your book. You can sell the book using media advertising or you could allow a charity to sell the books for you and allow them to collect some or all of the proceeds from the sales. If the books are small, they are frequently given out for free at various venues in the target area. Try to have a way for your advertising companies to monitor how much new business your book has brought into their business. This will make a great marketing pitch for solicitation to other businesses.

Coupons mailings

Type: Part time
Startup costs: Low
Location: Dedicated home space

We get them all the time in the mail. An envelope comes stuffed with coupons for discounts and two-for-one offers. This business goes out and solicits other businesses to pay them to send out the coupons to hundreds or thousands of potential customers. The business is very localized and focuses on neighborhood businesses that may draw all of their customers from a limited neighborhood. There are franchises in this sector, but this is a local business and franchises will not have an advantage over your operation.

Make sure you understand the postage rates for the mailing. Putting in one or two more coupons may set you into the next weight limit for the mailing and eat up a lot of your profits.

You will have to meet with the potential business prospects many times to get their business.

Courier

Type: Part time
Startup costs: Low
Location: Home based

Attorneys and large businesses are always using people with cars to transport urgent documents for signatures around town. You can be their courier and hand-carry any small parcels they request. They may use you over the major services in your town if they want you to wait for a response or signature. Focus on finding one or two business customers.

You will have to provide your business card to the right people in companies who make these types of arrangements. Franchises in this sector do not have an advantage over you.

Make contact directly with the businesses that would consider using you. Check and upgrade your vehicle insurance to cover this activity.

Cruise experts/speakers

Type of business: Lifestyle
Startup costs: Low
Location: On the cruise ship

Cruise ships are frequently looking for specially trained people such as nurses and doctors to travel on board. They also like experts to lecture and teach. Experts in archeology are used for cruises that visit many of the archeological sites in Mexico. Learn about the ancient history of Greek culture and teach in English or another language on cruises of this area. Use your imagination. This is a little known business that makes more travel fun than money.

You might want to set up your own tour using a cruise ship. The ship will normally provide the space for you to do your lectures. You can work with a museum or charity to sell the extra service cruise. You might get a group discount that will pay for your cruise and some money on the side. You might also make a fair amount of money from setting up those side trip land excursions. However, the cruise may not like you taking this business from them since a lot of their profits come from setting these side trips up.

There are limited cruise ship owners who will be your clients. You might also consider setting up a teaching and guided tour cruise that you can sell through a museum.

Data Mining

Type: Part time
Startup costs: Low
Location: Home based

Companies have needs for information today. It is easy to buy one of the CD-based business lists and have them sort through and find companies that meet a certain criteria. But it takes lots of time to do some detailed searches beyond the basic criteria. You may have to search the web and search the web site of every company that meets specific criteria to find out detailed information that your client may want about the company. Your client may not have the personnel to do this work or not want to pay their high labor costs to do the function. Services provide a lot of data to large companies but no one is servicing the smaller businesses well.

Some clients may have you calling other companies to get certain information that is not normally collected by the data services. The possibilities are endless for what information you can collect and how you collect it. If you develop a specific type of information you collect, you might be able to sell the same data to a number of companies.

This becomes a nice home-based business working from a computer or calling on the telephone using the cheaper residential/home office long distance phone rates. Make sure all of the techniques that you use to gather information are legal. Data mining is being looked at now for new regulations to control what these information gatherers collect.

Contact companies directly who may have need for your service.

Digital Keepsakes

Type: Part time
Startup costs: Medium
Location: Home based

As technology changes, people will want to maintain their keepsake photographs and videos on DVDs or whatever future storage media comes along. The equipment is not too expensive but if you use professional quality equipment, it is probably not worthwhile to purchase the equipment for your own family's quantity. Set up a business with top quality equipment that will produce good output. Mix in music and headings. You should be able to put together a better quality product than the large retailers doing this in bulk quantities using a fixed format.

Check out the latest things that the franchises and large retailers are offering. Specialize in the custom touch.

The baby boomers probably have the most quantity of these older technologies to update. You may have better access to this market. Let independent drugstores and not-for-profit groups do your sales. Or you can try traditional print advertisement to find the customers.

Disposables sales

Type: Part time
Startup costs: Low to medium
Location: Home based or set up a shop. You need storage space such as a barn but you can also rent self-storage units.

Many businesses use a lot of disposables such as latex gloves, plastic bags and protective clothing. While supply companies serving a specific industry have the big businesses covered, they may not be covering the small neighborhood stores. Put together a number of products and service the small guys with excellent delivery, service and a wide selection.

Remember in this business, you can gain a new customer forever if you can provide them a stock of what they need in an emergency. Advertise in industry specific publications in your area and brochures sent to the businesses in your area.

Document destruction

Type: Part time
Startup costs: Medium
Location: At the customer's location

You might see trucks for document destruction around the office district in your town. They service large offices that have documents with personal information on their clients or they have confidential company information that must not fall into the competition's hands. They do not use home shredders since they are not secure. They use specialized equipment to do total destruction and closely follow a rigid procedure to make sure destruction is complete.

This service is provided for big businesses. But there are hundreds of smaller businesses that are not doing the job that they should be doing. The large document destruction companies do not service single practitioner Doctor's offices, insurance agencies, and small offices. This is your market niche.

It will take a lot of effort to teach potential customers the risk and liability they are taking on if they just throw confidential information in the dumpster. There are a number of supply companies on-line that have the needed equipment for this business.

For marketing, develop a brochure that will provide the exact process that you will follow to dispose of the documents that you are assigned. Make sure you have a process that your customers can understand. Check into government regulations in certain industries that have to dispose of confidential information. Let your customers know if the are violating any regulations. They may require specific equipment and procedures. Make sure you follow your procedure to the letter. Watch any employee or subcontractor involved in your process. You may have to be bonded for some customers.

Document preservation-Personal

Type: Part time
Startup costs: Medium/high
Location: Dedicated space

Every family and business has those keepsake documents that they want to preserve. If they are framed in a standard picture frame, the keepsake will eventually yellow or deteriorate. News articles, pictures with celebrities, awards, and letters of recognition are just a few of the possibilities. Businesses may want to preserve their employee, supplier or customer recognition awards before they present them.

A small woodworking shop can build different sizes and shapes of plaques so these documents can be sealed and laminated onto solid wood or laminate-coated medium-density pressboard plaques for better preservation. The success in this business is all in the quality and design of your product. Customize to distinguish your product from others. Go to framing shops or check them online and you may find a variety of styles and materials that competitors in the business use.

Find a framing shop in a few different cities to sell your work. You cannot service competing framing shops in the same city unless they have a different clientele. You might be able to sell your product online

The documents are sent to you via UPS, FedEx or US Post Office and you return the product to the retailer the same way. You will have to have dedicated space with separate rooms for clean and dusty work. So the space will have to be larger than a garage or basement.

Depending on the sophistication of your offerings, expensive equipment may be required for professional edging.

Dog Kennels

Type: Part time
Startup costs: Medium
Location: Devoted building

Most people with dogs have had to use kennels. I know they are expensive to use but they are the only alternative if you don't have family or very good friends in town.

You can open a kennel and board dogs or cats when owners go on vacation. You have to work every day at it and while it will not be a full time job if you keep the number of animals down, it sure will be 7 days a week and a few hours three times a day. Consider carefully if you really want this type of business since it is a lot different than going to your neighbors house and feeding their cat every few days. Licensing requirements and zoning may be an issue.

But you may want to start in this sector by offering home watching and walking of pets for clients. Many clients would prefer this and it's a good way to see if you really like doing it.

Elderly moving

Type: Part time
Startup costs: Low
Location: Home based

When seniors move into independent living facilities, dependent living facilities or die, it frequently is a difficult situation for their children to handle. A lot of times it is hard trying to cut down on the bulk of their possessions. Garage sales may be needed to dispose of items or you may have to contact a number of used furniture dealers or antique shops. Packing items for moving and the moving itself must be done.

Providing these services as a turnkey operation can be a compelling business and it should be easy to capture business from people in your personal networks such as churches and civic organizations to which you belong. You can also consider advertising in senior's publications or contact independent living facilities and nursing homes so they can refer clients to you.

Make sure you keep good documentation on everything you sell for them and on how you priced each item. On the TV antique show you see every week, someone has bought a million dollar antique for $5 at an estate sale. Think of what your customers or customer's children will do if they see mom's heirloom on TV that you sold for $5. Make sure you are working with reputable moving companies.

Elderly services

Type: Part time
Startup costs: Low
Location: Home based

The elderly, living by themselves, frequently require a lot of help from their in-town children. Provide these services when the children go on vacation or take some of the load off the children all year. Doctor's appointment transportation, medicine pickups, laundry, house cleaning, food pickup and bill paying are some of the areas you might consider. Check out the numerous franchises in this sector to see what services they are offering. Transportation may require special licensing. Remember that you are working with the elderly and special care considerations will be needed for some of your clients.

Many seniors' publications may be good advertising space for this type of business. But don't forget to target the senior's caretakers/ family members also.

Embroidery

Type: Part time
Startup costs: Medium
Location: Dedicated space at home

Today's embroidery machines/computers are really amazing. You can take a colored insignia and turn that into an embroidery program to decorate hundreds of clothing items. While the machines are fairly expensive, they are relatively small now.

Find a few companies and cater to their needs. Contact them directly. Contact not-for-profit organizations to put together a series of products they can sell to members as a fundraiser. Work through sewing shops as your retail agents.

Check out the franchises in this sector to see what they are offering but they don't have an advantage over you for small local business and not-for-profit work.

Ethnic or geographic publications

Type: Part time
Startup costs: Medium
Location: Home based or an office in the target area

Think about an ethnic group in your town. Put together a publication of articles, leaders profiles, news and coming events focused entirely on that community. Get your advertisements from businesses servicing that community. Focus on a limited area so the franchises will not have an advantage over you. This works better for people of the specific ethnic group or who are known in the geographic location.

Think of a neighborhood known by its location. Most cities have certain neighborhoods that flourish on their identity. Put together a publication for tourists who come to that area. You can also focus the publication to the locals who live and work there so they will get a better sense of community. This business requires a lot of door-to-door contact with advertisers along with mailings to potential advertisers.

Expense Reduction Analyst

Type: Part time
Startup costs: Low
Location: Home based

Large companies have people constantly looking into how much they are paying for everything they purchase. Small companies skip over this point and stick with their routine vendors. You can provide this expense reduction analysis service for them. There is a lot of literature on this type of business on-line and at the library but the hard part is taking every major expense and finding out if there are cheaper alternatives. This involves a lot of calling and checking. Once you start identifying the basic low-cost suppliers of common items, the work goes a lot quicker.

There are franchises in this area but some of them are really trying to get the customers to buy through the franchise's buying group that is a big profit center for the franchise. They may not always be interested in finding the best price for the customer. So stay independent and loyal to your customer's needs. Advertise your service in local business journals.

Fall cleanup aide

Type: Seasonal
Startup costs: Medium
Location: Home based

Fall requires leaf removal from gutters, lawns and plant beds. Some equipment is helpful in doing the work but anyone can do the work by hand. Your business can be a success since these are dangerous tasks that people don't want to do, especially those tasks involving climbing up on ladders. Raking of leafs can be a big job without power blowers. But you can afford the power blowers if you provide this service to a number of customers. Also pruning of certain plants is required at this time and cutting back of the perennials.

The hard work here may exceed many people's capabilities. You are working on ladders and working with power equipment.

Pass out circulars or brochures door-to-door in a targeted area.

Fence and mailbox installer

Type: Part time
Startup costs: Low to medium
Location: Home based

Fencing and roadside mailboxes are available at every discount home improvement store. But there are hundreds of other designs and manufacturers that are not represented through these channels. Pick up a few different lines of these products that are different from the ones you see at the major stores. Buy a power augar so you can easily dig the deep holes required that are difficult for the average home do-it-yourselfer to do. Find a high traffic location to put up a variety of fences that you would like to sell and install them with a sign for your business.

It may be better to hire someone to do the installation work while you do the sales and pricing.

Advertising in local media is necessary. Send a letter to your product suppliers so they will know that you will professionally install their products. They may pass along references from calls they get.

Festival Organizer

Type: Seasonal
Startup costs: Medium to high
Location: Home based

There are all types of festivals. You may have been to a certain type of festival while you were on vacation in another city. Does your area have this type of festival? If not, why not start one. Art festivals, farmers equipment festivals, neighborhood specific festivals, ethnic and cultural festivals, festivals around a historic event or location in your area are all ideas that can lead to a success. For children there could be kite festivals, clown festivals or festivals around certain playing games.

Start small, renting a few tents for booths and grow each year. Obtain fees for booth rentals, parking and admissions. Food vendors are always a big part of these festivals so don't forget to contact them to rent space.

Most types of festivals will have a unique set of clients who attend. Look into what media they are getting their information from and utilize advertisements there. Contact the media that covers your clientele and put out notices about your event. All of the newspapers have free listings of weekend events. Contact them early so they will put out notices of your event.

This work is concentrated on the weeks leading up to your event. But a lot of the work happens months before the event occurs finding vendors to attend. So don't be surprised by the amount of up front work required for this business.

Special event insurance is available to reduce much of this risk and should be mandatory for you.

Financial planning

Type: Part time
Startup costs: Low
Location: Home or office based

If your expertise is in the financial area, you may want to consider financial planning as your second career. You may be employed by one of the large companies in this field or you may be working as an independent contractor for a smaller local firm. Some groups may want you to get certification to work for them and selling certain products may require licensing in different states. Focus on people you know and on people of your age group who will consider you more mature than the young people who also enter this field.

Proven expertise and training/qualification programs by the large certification organizations are needed to gain customer's confidence. In most areas this will require licensing if you are working with certain products for your customers.

There are a number of franchises in this sector that set up large practices. It is fine to work for them but they are big businesses that require full time work to run. Work for others or start a small practice devoted to people nearing retirement that you know or have a common bond with such as a church or civic groups.

You will either need to start advertising or join an existing business that does the marketing while you do the financial planning. Satisfied customers' referrals are the way you will build your business.

Fitness and health products

Type: Part time
Startup costs: Medium
Location: Home based or store

This product line is called out separately since you can focus on certain types of products that are specific to your age group, avoiding the mass-marketed items for all age groups. Showing your well-preserved body can be a great implied selling point for your products and convince others about their benefits without making unsupportable statements. So pick on someone your own age where you have a natural advantage to convince them.

There are a number of franchises, distributorships, and MLM marketers in this business. Choose who you want to sell for carefully.

Floral Preservation

Type: Hobby business
Startup costs: Low
Location: Home based or sell through retail shops

Picking wild flowers, garden flowers or any type of plants or leafs and stabilizing them so they will last for a long time, is the hobby of some. Arranging them in vases, frames or in unique arrangements can make a very sellable product that you can sell at festivals or through small retailers. You should probably be seriously into this hobby if you want to enter it as a business.

Food preparation for specialty diets

Type: Part time
Startup costs: Medium
Location: Storefront or home based

If you would like to cook up meals for others, focus on the special diet customers. Salt free, sugar free, fat free, gluten free diets abound with little choice available in the prepared food section of the grocery stores. Professional packaging equipment is required to get into this business but it isn't very expensive. Check your local food preparation laws and the packaging and labeling regulations if you start this business. You may have to work as personal chefs to those people to make this work without a food production license. Working out of home and delivering the products to the customer keeps costs down.

You may need a professional dietician or a lot of expertise to develop the menu and specific recipes for the products. Make sure you are following your approved recipes that have been developed with expertise in the area.

There may be some organizations for people with medical problems that necessitate special diets that would be a great place to advertise.

Food Stands

Type: Seasonal
Startup costs: Medium to high
Location: Mobile or rented

This is similar to operating a restaurant and requires the same skills and licenses. But you will need to find a seasonal location where a year around restaurant will not work out and get a lease that you will only have to pay during the busy season. You might set up a trailer kitchen and move that to busy locations and just set up picnic tables around your location for the season.

Using a mobile kitchen or trailer will keep startup costs down. There are franchises that offer this equipment and there are suppliers that just offer the trailers without any ongoing franchise commitment from you.

If you are at a mobile location in a busy area or move around to festivals or recreation areas, you have captive customers and will only require good signage to market yourself.

Fractional Ownership

Type: Hobby
Startup costs: Low
Location: Home based

People can't or don't want to spend the money to buy some of the high priced luxury recreational items but do want access to them on a whim. Set up a fractional ownership program on your favorite hobby such as sailboats, RV's, airplanes or even resort condominiums. Get a number of people to buy into your group to cover the cost of buying the item and charge them a monthly fee to use it a limited number of hours on a fixed or sign up schedule. Let them pay for extra time, as it is available. Each will pay a monthly fee for the ongoing maintenance costs. As the number of people in a group grows, you can purchase multiple units and the scheduling and desirability become better.

There is at least one franchise in this area in the sailing sector so check it out to see what they offer. Charge a small monthly administration fee for your efforts of taking care of the group and the equipment. Do some of the repair and maintenance yourself to collect additional fees. But the big advantage is that you may be able to use the equipment for your favorite hobby when others are not using it.

Advertise in a newsletter or magazine of that particular focus. Go to general aviation airport hangers or marinas and post a notice there. They will normally let you do that if they think you will maintain your equipment at their facility.

Fun Education

Type: Part time
Startup costs: Low
Location: Work at customer's premise

Put together a program to make education fun. You might find some franchises for fun demonstrations of science principals or you may find "challenges of knowledge" built into a game show format. Check out their information on-line. Develop a program for a specific school grade and have interschool competition or develop an in-class program. Provide educational science shows to schools and for parties. This is a mix between entertainment and education.

Market certain types of programs to schools. Day care centers may be right for your level of program. Children's publications may be the right media to advertise in if you service birthday parties.

Fundraising Packager

Type: Part time
Startup costs: Medium
Location: Home based

Every not-for-profit organization is looking for fundraising ideas. Most don't have enough volunteers to organize and do all of the back room work needed for product sales. But if you walk into an organization, especially one that you are already active in, and have a package of products that you can deliver to them, they might want to sell these as a fundraiser.

You will buy, put together and deliver to the sales people the exact number of products they will be selling or have pre-sold. All the organization must do is have their members sell the products and deliver them. You take care of the rest.

Special baskets for certain holidays may be an ideal starting point for your business. Contact charities, churches and youth groups as potential customers.

Garden curbs

Type: Part time/seasonal
Startup costs: Medium
Location: Home based

Many people love using those concrete garden curbs in various colors and patterns instead of the black plastic separators that you buy at the garden shops. It takes a piece of equipment and a little training to get you into this business. There are comprehensive franchises in this area. There are also equipment suppliers that provide training for people who purchase their equipment without further obligations like a franchise requires.

Gain a lot of your business by subcontracting with landscaping contractors to do this work for them. Advertise in gardening publications for your area. Post circulars or your card at every garden shop in your area

Garden Products

Type: Home based
Startup costs: Low
Location: Large home garden

If you grow fruits, vegetables or nuts, you could be selling them at the local public market. This isn't for the small backyard gardener with a dozen extra tomatoes. You will have to have large quantities of product to make it worthwhile to pay the vendor fees and transport it to market. Try selling your products at a local public market near you before going to the larger regional markets.

You might consider setting up a roadside stand if you have a busy street location to use. Sometimes small grocery stores will buy your product or some restaurants may deal with you if you have a wide variety of products or if you have a specialty product, like heirloom tomatoes, that they cannot get from their food distributors. If you are growing flowers, try making the rounds of flower shops some mornings to see if they will buy your products.

Not really a farmer? The public markets have a lot of resellers of products such as spices, honey and condiments. Jump in and try these.

Geocaching Games

Type: Hobby
Startup costs: Low
Location: Home based

If your hobby is geocaching, you may find ways to profit from setting up courses and hunts for others. Consider contacting a charity or not-for-profit group to organize an outing for their members or as a fundraiser. Maybe a business will use this as a team building exercise for their management. You may be able to set a course paid for by advertisers that put coupons about their business at the cache locations. You might consider long distance travel searches and get local motels or campsites along the way to provide discounts for the traffic.

You might rent out equipment and have an introductory course in the GPS use for some of these adventures.

Contact charities and other not-for-profits to see if they would like to set up a fundraiser around your course. Make a geocoin for their event so participants will have a collectible from the event.

Gift Baskets for Special Occasions

Type: Seasonal
Startup costs: Medium
Location: Home based

Put together gift baskets for special holidays and this business becomes seasonal. The full time providers normally have a storefront and have to provide special baskets for every holiday and general ones year around to cover their overhead. Focus on a specialty basket. Sell it through a general retailer, paying them a fair percentage of the sale price. Send out mailings or drop off circulars at homes. Put advertisements in local newspapers.

Work with not-for-profits for them to sell these as a fundraiser. Advertise in local media at the time of year you are selling the baskets.

Hobby finished products

Type: Hobby
Startup costs: Low
Location: Home dedicated space

Selling the output of your favorite hobby is a dream that many people may have for supplemental income. Too many people find that this just doesn't work out. But if you try focusing on making sure your product looks different from the mass produced items, customizing the product for the individual customers, focusing on niche groups (such as making the complex designs of bonsai pots instead of general bowls and vases), and making sure you have someone to retail your product for you, you may be able to provide a supplemental income from this business. If you don't want to spend more time at various fairs selling your product than you do making the product, make sure you find someone else to retail the products for you.

Start by using your hobby equipment instead of running out and buying the heavy, commercial equipment that may be needed if you are successful. Sell your product through other businesses and at festivals. Consider selling through a table concession at hobby or neighborhood festivals and special events. Setting up a storefront and regular advertisements add high fixed costs and should not be attempted until you really see how big the market is for your product

Your homeowner's insurance will not cover this work since it is now a business. So make sure you contact them to upgrade your coverage.

Hobby supplies

Type: Hobby
Startup costs: Medium
Location: Home based or Internet based

Supply materials to other hobbyists either at conventions or through an on-line store. Carry different products and more customized lines that the large hobby stores don't carry. Only open a storefront after you have too much business to handle through a home based business.

Advertise in hobby magazines only.

Holiday items

Type: Seasonal
Startup costs: Medium
Location: Home based or storefront

Costumes, party packages and specialty food preparation are used for holidays every month of the year. Cash in on these holidays such as St. Patty's Day, Halloween, Independence Day, Valentine's Day and Thanksgiving, to name a few.

You may be able to rent an empty storefront for a few weeks if you will allow the building owner to continue trying to rent the space and evict you with short notice. You can also sell products out of your house.

Advertise in local media at the time of the year you are servicing.

Home delivery of heavy products

Type: Part time
Startup costs: Medium to high
Location: Home with a large garage, barn or self-storage rental unit to store your inventory.

There are franchises and independent businesses that deliver dog food and swimming pool chemicals to your home. They anticipate when you are running low on supply based on your past use frequency and check with you for their next delivery. This allows them to service you a few days ahead of running out so they can make up more efficient delivery routes. Many times they charge no more than the stores do for the products because the saving of not having a storefront offsets the delivery costs.

The competitive advantage you are using is eliminating the heavy lifting for the customer. You may hire others to do the delivery and you run the business end. This may also allow you to not invest in a heavy-duty truck to deliver the items at the beginning until you see your success.

Advertising is a must in this business. Specify in your ads for your company that you will be doing the heavy lifting. Certain products may have specific magazines that you can advertise in. Telemarketing is the main method of sales but expect to make 20 or more calls for each initial sale you get.

Home-made food products

Type: Part time
Startup costs: Minimal
Location: Sell at markets and festivals

Sell your homemade food products at various festivals, markets and on your street. Check carefully into what is allowed in your area and what type of license may be needed. This could be canned and jarred condiments, pickled products, or jellies, and any fresh made products such as pies and other baked goods. Check into product labeling requirements. Use a certified kitchen to make your product, if required, or have some small company with approved facilities make your product for you.

If you travel around to festivals, you will not need to do advertising.

Home spring cleaning

Type: Seasonal
Startup costs: Low
Location: Home based

Try spring cleanup for basements and homes. This can be a nice short season job for some people. Look for customers that are extremely busy at this time or who are less physically able to do this heavier work.

Pass out circulars to homes in your target area. Try some neighborhood publications for advertising.

House sitter

Type: Lifestyle or part time
Startup costs: Low
Location: Home based

There are two types of house sitting. The first is where you go live in someone's house while they are gone and watch the property and possibly do some of the domestic chores and pet watching. This is a lifestyle business and doesn't make much money but can provide you with interesting locations to live for a while. There are publications and on-line sites that can help you set up these engagements.

There are also a number of condominiums where people live part of the year. In some cases, they may rent out their property when they are not there. If you live in that complex or near it, you might be hired to periodically check their unit. If things need attention, you will manage or do the work yourself. If they rent it out, you may do the cleanup between renters. Frequently you will find newsletters for these housing groups to advertise in or they may allow you to post a notice in a public area to find customers. Make sure your agreement is worded adequately and reviewed by an attorney to relieve you of liability to the property while you are watching it.

House swap coordinator

Type: Part time
Startup costs: Low
Location: Home based

Many magazines offer house swaps between different parties. This is a great business that will see a lot of growth in the future as the baby boomers' desire to travel around and experience living in other parts of the country or in other countries for a few months at a time without spending a lot of money.

The big on-line companies and magazines do a credible job catering to these people. New companies will continue to enter this sector in the future as the market grows. But if you focus your business, you may find a niche where you can excel above the larger players.

Your church may have a lot of parishioners who would consider a house swap with members of the same denomination in other cities or countries. Or your city may have a lot of people who want to swap with specific other cities, such as sister cities, that you can focus on. Target advertisements in publications that cater to your specific clientele.

Watch the wording of your contracts and informational brochures to ensure you are not held liable for any unfortunate circumstances.

How-to videos

Type: Part time
Startup costs: Low
Location: Home based

If you have some real expertise and do not want the ongoing responsibility of teaching your expertise to others through classes, try putting together a how-to video on the subject. You will have to work out exactly what and how you are going to say and teach everything before making the video. This can't be completed ad lib.

Every city has a number of companies that regularly make videos for advertisements, corporate training and infomercials. They will make a far superior product than what you can do with a friend on the other end of a home camera.

You sell your product on-line or through organizations that cater to your skills. Run a small mail order service to sell them out of your home from a web site or phone calls.

You must find a skill that is too difficult for a lot of people to understand from sketches drawn in books about the subject. There are a lot of areas where I just can't understand what the how- to books are trying to do without actually seeing someone do it.

Ice cream shop

Type: Seasonal
Startup costs: Medium to high
Location: Short term rental or a trailer

Set up a summer location for an ice cream or dessert spot in a vacant storefront in a busy location. If you can find a vacant place, you can try to talk the landlord into a 3 or 4-month lease. Keep any decoration or equipment to a minimum and use things that are removable so you can go to a different location next season. An unheated location may be available which is not suitable for year around use. You can set up a location using a trailer and picnic tables.

Advertisement may be necessary for a permanent location or you can rely on moving your trailer to where the captive customers are congregating.

Industrial equipment maintenance

Type: Lifestyle
Startup costs: Low
Location: You find work wherever you go

You could have a nice lifestyle business if you learn to repair a specialized type of equipment that few people have. You will go to the industrial sites to do the repair and tune-ups. Items like repairs of sheet metal brakes are a perfect item for this business. Pack your RV and travel wherever you want. Make a few calls to people in the city where you are going a few days before you arrive to get some business together.

Inflatables

Type: Part time
Startup costs: Medium to high
Location: Home based

There are businesses that buy inflatable games for children to bounce on and rent them for parties, festivals and businesses' special events. It is heavy work to set one of these up for just a few hours of use. You can rent this equipment from various rental businesses to try the business out before you make a large investment in your own inflatables. You could also set up a number of inflatable games in an indoor location for the winter and keep it open on the weekends and by reservation for parties. Check out what the franchises in this sector are offering.

There are inflatable figures of people and products that you can rent out as attention grabbers and advertisement in front of businesses. Even tethered blimps can attract a lot of people for an opening. Your customers may not want to invest in their own equipment so they may hire you to locate something outside their new store to attract attention.

Advertising is critical for parties and winter locations. If you are operating children's activities at events and festivals, you have a captive audience and do not need to advertise. Contact new businesses for the advertising type inflatables.

Information center/kiosk

Type: Part time
Startup costs: Low
Location: Home office

In many hotels, rest stops, gasoline stations, tourist attractions and tourist information offices, you will find displays of informational brochures for recreation venues, restaurants and tours. Setting these up and monitoring them can be a good business if you get the businesses involved to pay you a fee to have their brochures in multiple locations and keep those centers stocked.

Directly contact tourist attractions to put their brochures in your information centers. You must also contact hotels, rest stops and some of the same tourist attractions personally to allow you to put your information centers in their locations.

International flight courier

Type: Lifestyle
Startup costs: Minimal
Location: Home office

Occasionally, you see companies advertising for couriers to take items to distant locations using the courier's luggage quota. They will pay for your ticket and sometimes a stipend for you to deliver the items to a client or to an office they may have in that location. You can't take much of your own luggage but it is a free or inexpensive trip. You must travel when they need you.

There are magazines and web sites that allow you to post your availability for these services. You may also want to contact some of the large international companies to offer your service. Know whom you are carrying items for and make sure they are reputable companies so you do not get caught bringing things that are forbidden in those countries.

Janitorial

Type: Part time
Startup costs: Low
Location: Home office

Offices hire people to come to their premise, in the evening or on weekends, to clean up the area and empty the trash. Limit your hours by limiting the size of your contracts. Contact those 3 and 4 person operations since bigger services probably have contacted the larger offices.

Advertise in business magazines for the local area. Send mailings to companies in your area and follow each one up with a personal call to the responsible person in that organization.

Make sure any people you hire are honest since you will be held responsible for any missing items.

Jewelry sales

Type: Part time
Startup costs: Medium
Location: Home based

Doing this as a home-based business is becoming quite popular. There are numerous suppliers of unique jewelry designs that you won't find in the chain stores. You may have customers come to your house, sell at parties in customer's homes, or sell at various festivals. Look for a line that is unique from what you see others selling. There are many MLM groups selling this way.

You could start with a small amount of inventory and build up as you get more confidence in your business. Start building a client list for mailings from day one. Send out fliers for a grand opening sale.

Liquidators of personal property

Type: Part time
Startup costs: Low
Location: Home office with garage space

Many families do not have the time to liquidate the physical assets of their parents when their parents die. It may take weeks or months to get rid of the furniture, appliances, clothing and other personal items. It might take a few weeks to get everything ready for a garage sale with the limited time people have today. All the time, the estate may be paying rooming rent that might exceed the value of the assets. Someone can go in on a day's notice, empty the premise, move it back to a garage or warehouse and liquidate the items more cost effectively than the family putting in all of the work.

Adverting in senior oriented publications is a good start. Make sure that you get reasonable prices for the items so you don't sell the missing Picasso for $5, thinking it is just a cheap poster.

Mail, re-mail, internal mail sorting and fulfillment services

Type: Part Time
Startup costs: Minimal
Location: Dedicated home space

If you have that basement area free, you may be able to start a mailing business of your choice.

Many of these web-based retail companies and some marketing companies may want you to store their products or literature and they will have your computer print out labels so that you can send the correct product to their customers. You may need to buy or rent postage machines to process this type of work. Contact your target companies directly.

Some large or mid sized businesses that have multiple locations may hire you to sort and deliver their internal mail. Contact management at your target company and provide them with some superior service angles and cost savings they can use to justify your services.

This may take a fair amount of dedicated space in your home for storage of the fulfillment items and space for processing. Make sure you are insured to cover any damage that happens to the inventory. Check zoning to make sure this is allowed from your house. Make sure you do not violate any postal regulations by delivering corporate mail for the company.

Marketing for small companies

Type: Part time
Startup costs: Minimal
Location: Home office

Most small businesses don't have a marketing department. Be their marketing department "on-call" and help them put together grand-openings, clearance sales, coupon programs and co-branding if your expertise is in this area. Walk into a potential customer with a small program design so they will be able to understand the impact you can have on improving their sales. Have connections for those special attractants for these events such as spotlights and inflatable games and advertisements.

There are now a few franchises that serve this sector. Check them out on line to see their offerings and pricing.

Medical Auditor

Type: Part time
Startup costs: Minimal
Location: Home office

People don't understand medical bills, especially hospital bills. It is difficult to figure out what services they were charged for unless they understand the codes the biller uses. They also have to figure out what is covered by their insurance plan and what should be that wasn't covered. It is difficult to know which insurance plan will provide them with the best coverage based on the medications they use and which they may need in the future. Check out what services are being offered by the franchises in this sector.

While things are changing rapidly at the time of this writing, there will always be a need for someone who has reviewed the bills many times and understands the process to help those less able. Start your business performing this function for others. You can charge a fixed hourly fee or try to obtain a percent of the found saving for your fee. Advertise in local media and possibly focus on senior's publications.

It may take a few bill reviews to learn the proper billing codes and procedures before you will make a profit large enough to warrant spending the amount of time needed. Once you get through the learning curve, you can do this relatively quickly.

Mobile oil change

Type: Part time
Startup costs: Low to medium
Location: Home based

Provide oil changes, car washes and minor repairs for customer's cars at their home or office location. Some larger employers may actually help you and allow you to advertise in their employee newsletter to save their employees from having to skip out early to get these things done. Look into health club or grocery store parking lots to provide this service or any place you can take care of the oil change while they are inside shopping.

Check out what the franchises in this sector are offering and charging. Start small using your vehicle and perform minor services that require little equipment. Build up your business and then consider a dedicated truck that will allow you to transport tools and supplies to do more difficult work. Advertise with a sign on your truck to get noticed in the parking lots where you are working. Get on a regular schedule at these locations so people will expect you to be at that location at a specific time. Pass out windshield flyers at business or health club parking lots.

If you perform these services at people's homes, you will need to advertise in local media.

Mold testing

Type: Part time
Startup costs: Low
Location: Home based

Home and business testing for mold, radon and other dangerous pollutants is quite easy and can be performed after a little training. Don't get involved in clean up and remediation work unless you know what you are doing. Stick with only collecting the testing samples and have a list of remediation contractors who will provide you a referral fee if you refer your clients with problems. You do not want to process the samples yourself. That requires certified laboratories. Make sure your agreements and brochures state clearly that you do not process the samples.

Advertise in local media. Contact building inspection companies and offer this service to them with some referral fee back to them. Some of these companies do the testing and some do not.

Work through organizations to offer their members group discounts or a donation back to them if they recommend your service to their members. Contact real estate agents to let them know about your services and offer them a referral fee.

Non-medical services for elderly, disabled or busy patrons

Type: Part time
Startup costs: Low
Location: Home based

Home cleaning, cooking, errands, shopping, transportation and paying bills are some of the services that you should consider providing for elderly or disabled customers. This is a rapidly growing sector and will grow in the future as more people get into their retirement years. There are a number of franchises in this sector so check out what services they are offering. Check into licensing requirements for handling money or transporting your customers.

Getting this business going will require a lot of advertising in senior's publications. Put up posters for your business at any place seniors or disabled people congregate. Get your name out to charitable and service organizations that work with your customers.

Old fashion skills

Type: Hobby/part time
Startup costs: Low
Location: Home based

If you know old fashion skills such as woodworking/cabinetry, cobbling, growing unique heirloom produce, leatherwork or the likes, you can teach others your skills. Look for craft shops to host your training sessions or set up a garage workshop where you can host a few students at a time.

Market your classes utilizing posters at craft stores if you are using their facilities to provide the training or if you will recommend that your students buy the supplies necessary at that store. Advertise in local media.

On-site computer support

Type: Part time
Startup costs: Low
Location: Home based

We probably have all had the experience of being requested to disconnect and bring in our computer to the repair shop to get the hardware or software straightened out. Many people will pay the extra fare to have someone come to their house to take care of their computer problems. If your expertise is in computers, you might want to consider this as your business. You might work with others doing this business if their skills are in different sectors of repair and form an alliance. Ongoing training is essential to this type of business.

Advertise in local media. Put up posters in senior communities or condominium complexes.

Opener/closer

Type: Part time
Startup costs: Low
Location: Home based

Many absentee business owners are looking for someone who will open and close their business and may be looking for someone more mature than their regular help to empty the change machine or cash register. Look into laundromats, self-service car washes, convenience stores and the likes where the owner isn't working every day. This is an hour a day job working for someone else. Identify potential businesses in your target sector and area that might need this service and contact them directly.

Organizers

Type: Part time
Startup costs: Low
Location: Home based

In today's busy word people don't have the time and frequently don't have the skill to organize the spaces where they work and live. The right person with these skills can organize workspace, home offices, basements, garages, closets, kitchens or any other part of the house. You can make money by charging a flat fee for your design and labor and collect additional fees if you sell and install products to help them organize.

But don't limit your offerings to closet organization like many of the franchises. They are really in the business of selling storage products just providing more storage space and not really organizing anything.

Advertise in local media and provide small gift for word-of-mouth referrals

Outdoor activities

Type: Seasonal
Startup costs: High
Location: At your property location

If you have hundreds of acres of land in a great fishing or hunting location, you can turn this asset into a real business. You can charge other people for use of your land for these activities along with camping, hiking and making money from the associated camp store that sells everything they may need for any of these activities.

Only go into this sector if you already own the perfect property. You need to be open only for the peak time for your property.

There is at least one franchise in this sector that allows you to join a national network, which brings in customers from other such businesses.

Focus your advertising in the media for the recreation you are sponsoring.

Pamphlet publishing

Type: Hobby
Startup costs: Low
Location: Home based

If your hobby is history, local history or any other particular subject that is location specific, publish a small book or pamphlet on the matter of local interest. Historic drives or walks with a written or CD history lesson may sell well and attract newspapers to write stories about your product to spread the word. You will need to place the pamphlet in retail stores in the particular area you are talking about and you can also advertise them in tourist publications.

Consider publishing a starters guide for your favorite hobby. Focus on advertising in hobby publications and for hobby pamphlets. Try to place them in craft stores.

Self-publishing your pamphlet and selling it directly to retailers is the way to start. On-line you will find a number of companies that will print your paperback book inexpensively and print them on-demand so you can purchase them in small quantities.

Party host

Type: Part time
Startup costs: Low
Location: Home based

Specialize in children's parties. Find activities that you can do at the party. Some of these activities may take equipment that is too expensive to buy for one party but you can afford to buy it since you are throwing a party every weekend. Crafts and art activities are also popular for children's parties.

Try organizing special activity parties for adults. There are suppliers of funny hat kits that can be used as a theme for a party. New theme party ideas take a lot of time to track down and order and frequently overwhelm someone who is spending the time for just one party. But you can track down a number of ideas and put them into your party offering booklet, spending the time once and planning many parties for that idea.

You can take care of all of the food and beverage arrangements to take the load off of the host. Pass out your card and brochure at every party.

Personal trainer/Fitness trainer

Type: Part time
Startup costs: Low
Location: Exercise club or go to client's home

If exercise is your specialty or hobby, try being a personal trainer for others. It may make a great part time job, especially if you get specialized training. Can you put together a tune up program before the winter for skiers? You can also try off-season training programs for devotees of a particular sport.

Set up classes for groups in tuning up for specific sports or provide group classes through any of the health clubs in your area. They may allow you to use their facilities and equipment at a nominal fee since this would allow them to show potential customers their facilities.

Check into licensing requirements especially if you are offering specialized service. There is also certification offered by a number of organizations after necessary training and testing. There are a number of franchises just entering this field. Start by offering a class at your neighborhood fitness center. Then branch out as you find loyal followers. Bringing mobile equipment to client's home is also a model you might consider but you will have higher startup costs and this will require a lot of physical effort to set it up at each client's home. But they will pay enough extra to cover the work.

Finding customers is mostly by word-of-mouth but use posters at the clubs or other appropriate locations especially if you focus on specific needs.

Plants, flowers or vegetables

Type: Seasonal
Startup costs: Low
Location: Home based

Sell all types of plants that you have started in your house, barn or greenhouse in spring at various public markets or farmer's markets. Sell fruits and vegetable plants that you have grown from seed at these same venues. Think about heirloom plants instead of the hybrids that the major farms grow. If you want to start trees, flowers or bushes, check my old friend out at freeplants.com since he runs a good small business on 1/8 of an acre house lot. You will have to start hundreds of flats of plants to make any money. Starting a dozens flats in a window just won't make much money.

Plant Renter

Type: Part time
Startup costs: Medium
Location: Home based with a greenhouse

Rent out plants to companies and rotate them around so each area gets a new look every few weeks or months. Take drooping plants out of their environment back to your green house to freshen them up before replacing them in the office.

Provide plants for placement in homes for special events that the owners may have or when they are trying to sell their house. Contact real estate agents, real estate staging companies and party planners for this business.

Maybe the company you are working with or the homeowner has a dead space at the end of a hallway or an unused corner. Develop a plan for a Japanese rock garden in that area that you can install for them. Try to rent or sell some of those indoor fountains or Zen fountains for the clients.

There are franchises in this sector. Check out their offerings and prices.

Poster/Picture Renter

Type: Part time
Startup costs: Low
Location: Home based

Rent out posters, art or motivational posters to commercial and industrial complexes. Move them around to give employees a different view. I remember looking at one motivational poster outside my office door for 5 years straight. It was nice but it would have been nicer to have a new one each month. Contact businesses directly with proposals to do their offices.

Printer Cartridge Refill

Type: Part time
Startup costs: Medium
Location: Home based

There have been cartridge refill businesses for years and this is now becoming even a bigger business. Refilling the ink dispensers that computer printers use is needed at every business and home. You can refill these at a fraction of the price of new cartridges with a small amount of equipment. Find a few mid-sized companies for clients and push the recycle aspect of the business as much as the money they can save. The home fill kits are not of high enough quality to satisfy most people.

Work with some charitable group to set up a fundraiser for them. Allow them to do the collection and the delivery while you do the refills.

The big office supply stores are now entering this sector but you can sell companies on your superior service and delivery. There are also a number of franchises but you can find the same equipment they use available through suppliers.

Product packager

Type: Part time
Startup costs: Low
Location: Home based

Many colleges offer to new students housing packages of items they will need for living in the dormitories. The package may include sheets, desk lamps and food items for new dormitory residents. If colleges in your area don't offer this, partner with them so they will mail out your brochure with the letters telling students where they will be housed for the next year. Share your revenue with the schools to get them to work with you.

Try putting together a hometown package. These make great gifts to send to past residents who have moved to other locations. Use those famous products for which your town is known. Offer them for sale at gift shops especially in the airports. Make them available to school reunion organizers for the out-of-town alumni.

Try putting together a package that a charity can sell for a fundraiser.

Publish your own book

Type: One shot
Startup costs: Low or medium
Location: Home based

I've seen self-published books on various subjects that people sell to their friends and in select locations. Children's activity books can help mothers keep their children busy on those rainy or snowy days. They may even help those grandparents find activities while babysitting their grandchildren when they don't have video games on their TV to keep the children amused. Different books are needed for each age level of child. These books can be reproduced on a copier and all you will need to buy or use is a binding machine. The local office supply store can provide this service.

Customize a book for the holidays by putting family members' face photographs into a pre-laid out book so young children can see their family members to better understand the subject matter. Out of town grandparents will pay the extra money to keep their face in their grandchildren's daily routine.

You might get into on-demand self-publishing of your book. You are reading a self-published book now. You will find plenty of companies that serve this market on-line. You pay for everything up front. They normally digitally print the books so small quantities can be printed at a time. But you still do most of the selling. Many of the self-publishers make the books available to the on-line retailers.

Take your book to the local bookstore or children's toy stores. After you see how it might sell, contact a distributor that these stores buy their books from. Charities may want to sell your book as a fundraiser. There are numerous books written on how to market your book.

Recognition awards/custom imprinting

Type: Part time
Startup costs: Medium
Location: Home based

Many companies still give out recognition awards and custom imprinted customer incentive products. A few suppliers are mass-producing these items in quantity but every town has a number of retailers that put the company's logo or the event date on the items using various printing techniques. This customization is what you can provide to companies from your basement while buying the main product from larger suppliers.

Larger imprinting companies frequently have high minimum purchases that the buyers need to order. You can distinguish yourself through lower minimums. Check out the product lines that full service stores offer as well as the items the franchises in this sector provide. But also look for unique products that no one else carries.

Sell through normal retail channels if your product is unique. If you are selling the same product that everyone else is selling, try putting together a small brochure and fax it to companies. Show how you can customize it differently from what your competition is doing.

Rock Hound

Type: Hobby
Startup costs: Low
Location: Home based

Yes, some people can make a nice supplemental income by collecting desirable rocks and selling them to others. If you know of a specific mineral location that is off limits to the public, you can try to obtain permission to collect there. The further away you sell from the source of the specimen, the more unique will be your offering.

A fossil collected from dry creek beds or quarries is another thing that you can offer.

There are a dozen known creeks and rivers and probably hundreds of unknown places where beautiful landscape rocks worth thousands of dollars are collected for Japanese Suiseki enthusiasts.

Don't count on this being a big money maker, but if you really get into the business and sell a number of items each year, your collecting travel trips may be a business expense.

Sell your product on-line, at festivals or hobby shows. Contact retailers who specialize in your type of rocks. Some of the large science education stores such as Wards will buy specimens as long as you have a large quantity of the same item.

Safety and security equipment for home and small business

Type: Part time
Startup costs: Medium
Location: Home based

Very few people will go into a store and go over to their safety and security equipment department. It is one of those sectors where people must see the product in their house or business and get a feel for how it will improve their lives. Smoke, fire, CO and security detectors are great products to sell although the discount houses offer these. You can do the installation for the customers to provide uniqueness over these low priced competitors. Also think about selling the mitigation equipment such as fire extinguishers and second story escape ladders. Door-to-door is the most effective way to sell your competitive advantage here. You can try to set up group discounts or fund raising programs for organizations if they will recommend you to their members or provide you with a forum to showcase your product to a large number of potential customers.

Fall-prevention home improvements are one area that can target seniors and bring a real benefit to those people who are your age.

One of the new areas that have spawn franchises and distributorships is fire proof products that will not burn like the conventional materials normally used. Look into these products as part of your offerings for building materials, fabrics and plastic components.

Seafood truck sales

Type: Seasonal
Startup costs: Medium to high
Location: Home based

In plaza parking lots in different parts of many cities, you can find refrigerated trucks selling seafood during one day of the week. The trucks sell only specific in- season items that are brought in fresh the night before from the east, west or gulf coast. Something is always in season. They don't have a large selection of items; so they must build up a reputation for having the freshest in-season products at a lower cost than the full service seafood stores in your town. They move around to different locations each day.

You might hire someone to make the truck runs over night and bring the fresh seafood to you to sell the next morning. You will have to make contacts with the boat captains or the large processors to get the best prices. Once you get the product back to your city, you can break the inventory down and load it onto a few smaller trucks to allow sales at various sites on the same day. You might also try public market locations.

You will have to advertise significantly if you want to gain new customers. Check into licensing requirements for this business.

Self-Storage

Type: Part time
Startup costs: High
Location: Must have a commercial site

You see self-storage units all over the country. But as any new area develops, new self-storage units will open up. You have to spend a lot of time and money opening one up and getting it filled. Most of the buildings are modular so you build one building of self storage units. When that building is filled, you build another building and so on.

In higher risk areas, these are manned whenever access is open. Frequently, employees from another business that you might own such as a gas station attendant, keeps their eye on who is going in and out. In rural areas, many are unmanned units with access limited through one gate that is continuously monitored by a camera.

You must understand the demographics of the people who use these facilities to find the good locations that will be a success. You will spend more time than you think evicting customers for non-payment. Have a professional look at the contract you have with your customers to head off liability for losses.

There are franchises and companies that offer pre-designed units that can help you find the better locations and provide you with financial plans and financing.

You will probably need to advertise in local media to get your initial customers but good signage on the buildings may be sufficient to get a few new customers to replace those that leave.

Seminar host

Type: Part time
Startup costs: Medium
Location: Home based

Set up seminars for various groups. Look into hobby skills or even business skills. Bring in nationally or locally known speakers in that field. Bring in writers of new books. Charge participants for attending the seminar and supplement your income by having a sales area selling books and tools for that interest. Rent hotel meeting spaces or community meeting rooms.

There are a number of franchises in this sector that cater to specific types of seminars. Check out what is being offered by others and see if they are working in your area. Do things that others are not doing in your area.

This will require a lot of advertising in specific media that caters to the type of seminar you are hosting.

Sewing Services

Type: Part time
Startup costs: Low
Location: Home based

Fabric stores are the place where many people start looking for what they want in curtains, bedding accessories or other household items made from fabrics. Most fabric shops now have custom services where they sell the material and design and subcontract out the sewing.

Focus on certain items or certain design styles and become the best at these products. Put together a book showing your work so the store that you subcontract to can show your work to their customers.

Contact a number of fabric retail stores and custom home decorators. Provide them with a book showing some of your best accomplishments.

While many home sewing machines are capable of doing the work, make sure you factor in more frequent replacement and repairs of the equipment if your business succeeds.

Sign shop in your basement

Type: Part time
Startup costs: Medium
Location: Home based

Sell your services on the web or through local advertisement. Most sign shop orders come in through fax or phone. They don't need to know you are a home-based business. You feed back the dimensions and layout to the client through e-mail or fax and then make up the sign in your basement. Most times you will deliver the sign or install it for the client at their desired location. Save all the overhead of a retail shop and undercut the competition's price.

Yes, there are a number of franchises in this sector but they require that you open a retail store and don't allow home-based businesses. But check out their web sites to see what services they offer.

This will require traditional advertising in local media.

Small motor and equipment repair

Type: Part time
Startup costs: Medium
Location: Home outbuilding

If you have the needed repair skills, start doing small motor and equipment repair. If you want a seasonal business, you can focus on one particular item such as snow blowers, lawn equipment, or outboard motors. If you want to make this more of a year around business you will have to move into multiple fields and do it all.

You will want to look into training and certification for repairs on some of this equipment. You will have to have proper building zoning to allow this as a home based business. Traditional advertising in the local media will be needed for this business.

Snowplowing

Type: Seasonal
Startup costs: High
Location: Home based

If you have a good pickup truck or SUV, you can add on a snow plow and clean driveways during the winter. This is big business frequently involving winter-long contracts in the northern states that see a lot of snow. But don't count this out as a nice supplemental business in more southern states where snowfall is less frequent. You will have to do it on an as-needed basis instead of having seasonal contracts.

Pass out circulars to homes in the area you want to service. In more southern areas that only need this service occasionally, have a refrigerator magnet to pass out to potential customers so they will always know how to contact you.

Much of your time and gas will be saved if you find many customers in a compact area. Doing driveways off of busy streets presents a lot higher accident risk. Make sure you have set up someone as a backup in case your equipment breaks and takes a few days to repair. The snow goes on whether you are ready or not.

Specialized car mechanic

Type: Part time
Startup costs: Low
Location: Rented space in a repair shop

Rent space in an existing repair shop. Finding a space with a side entrance so you will appear to have your own shop is even better. Specialize in the repair of one particular car and become more familiar with this car than the competition. Put your own sign up at your door so it won't feel like the much bigger repair shop where you are renting space. Create the identity as the specialist in your field. Certain classic cars have local publications that you can advertise in. Go to meetings of owner's groups.

Specialty industrial customer newsletter

Type: Part time
Startup costs: Low
Location: Home based

Put together a publication for customers of a certain business sector. Have generic articles teaching them about improvements in the industry, new equipment and safety with their products. Find a supply company in every town that will buy your generic publication. Customize part of the publication with advertisement and information about this customer's offerings and employees. Send the publication out to the list of their customers that they will provide to you.

You will have to do a lot of direct contact with companies that you want to provide with this product. Follow all copyright laws for information that you might find on the web.

Specialty industrial newsletter

Type: Part time
Startup costs: Low
Location: Home based

Do you know about a specific manufacturing sector? Put together a publication around this sector for your city. Sell advertisement to some of the companies that may have un-booked equipment time that they want to subcontract out. Maybe they have spare inventory of raw materials that they could sell to other companies. Put in articles about CEO's of the companies in your area, local training programs or economic development experts in how to grow the sector.

You will need to develop a list of businesses and the key people in those businesses who are in that industry. There are numerous companies that can provide you that list or you can use a phone book list. You will have to contact suppliers to that sector to sell advertising in your publication. Develop a mailing list for the finished newsletter or provide a newsstand at the places they work.

Specialty tools

Type: Part time
Startup costs: High
Location: Traveling show

There are some supply sectors with vans that travel to the business site to show off their product line. Develop a comprehensive array of products for different manufacturers and service locations that distributors do not service. Focus on equipment that the worker would like to feel and hold to check comfort before they buy it.

Safety shoes, personal safety equipment and hand tools are some of the areas that franchises and distributors have entered. There are some franchises in this area but you can sometimes assemble a more useful product mix on your own if you know the business you are serving.

You will have to contact companies directly and ask for their permission to show up in their parking lot and sell your products.

Spring cleanup aide

Type: Seasonal
Startup costs: Low
Location: Home based

Perform spring cleanup of residential yards. Get specialized rolling, turf grooming, and tree pruning equipment to do what your neighbors can't do themselves. Keep away from high cost equipment until you know you can support buying it.

Advertise in neighborhood publications, put up posters in key locations or pass out fliers in a door-to-door campaign.

Spring flower garden design and plantings

Type: Seasonal
Startup costs: Low
Location: Home based

Experienced gardeners could help others plan and plant their home gardens. Look in the upscale neighborhoods where they are more likely to hire professional contractors to do this.

Look for areas that traditionally have plantings such as rotaries and retailers' front green space. Think about putting together distinctive planters for storefront placement that will set off a particular neighborhood or community and market to all businesses in that area.

Develop a specialty if you want to get some business from general landscapers. You may decide that garden lighting is an expertise that you will develop. You can do the lighting for existing gardens and use this as the highlight of your gardens. On you can focus on water accents.

Get into this only if this is what you love doing. Keep a good photographic book of your accomplishments as your sales tool. Advertise in local media and contact homeowner associations directly.

Summer food sales

Type: Seasonal
Startup costs: Medium to high
Location: Mobile

Have a small kiosk, food cart, small vehicle, RV or a trailer set up to sell cooked food, ice cream or snack items at locations that attract the summer crowd such as busy parks, beaches and festivals. This may require a street vendor's license.

You will have a captive audience by your location so focus on good signage to attract customers.

Summer recreational equipment rentals

Type: Seasonal
Startup costs: Motorized equipment high, medium for other items
Location: Home based

Rent out beach chairs, umbrellas, inflatable water gear, boogie boards or even surf boards at ocean beaches, lakes and popular river locations.

You might want to rent out fishing boats, jet skis and ski boats in some recreation areas.

You will be at the location of the customer's use and you will have to attract them through signage and having the equipment out on display. Much of this is a spur of the moment decision for the customers.

Tax preparation

Type: Seasonal
Startup costs: Low
Location: Home based or a short-term rental space

There are free or inexpensive courses offered every year in most cities for tax preparation. This could put you in business for a month or two every year. Get out to the location of the customers instead of having them come to you. Maybe you can go to independent living facilities and nursing homes and develop special skills in tax preparation for the elderly. Set up a specific day or evening you are at a location so clients can plan on you being there.

Advertising will be necessary but look into local newsletters instead of the general media.

Telephone surveyor

Type: Part time
Startup costs: Low
Location: Home based

Surveyors gather information for large retailers who want to know their customers' desires. If your expertise is in market research, you can provide similar surveys for small business customers.

Contact the businesses you want as customers directly and put together a generic survey that you can do for them and show them how you will improve their business with the information you will gather.

If you run a home-based office, your telephone company may let you pay a residential rate for your phone calls and long distance saving considerably over commercial rates.

Theme publication

Type: Part time
Startup costs: Low
Location: Home based

If your expertise is in art, put together a monthly publication strictly on shops, shows, festivals and artists in the area. Plenty of shops will be willing to advertise in your bulletin.

You can consider a publication for the locals and tourists on festivals in your area.

Consider any of the following if they are of interest to you and have a high concentration in your area: general health, specific medical problems, environmental problems, local hiking trails, specific sports, water activities such as kayaking, surfing, fishing or rafting, religion, music scene, cooking or gardening. You will have to contact potential advertisers directly. You may want to place your publication at locations that sell products for your theme.

Tourists' maps

Type: Part time
Startup costs: Low to medium
Location: Home based

Develop a map for a particular tourist town or activity (like fishing) and place them at numerous tourist attractions. Sell advertising on this map and show the location of your paying customers' businesses more prominently on the map. It may cover a wine trail, fishing locations, or historic walking route or drive.

Check out what some of the franchises are doing nationally and see if something may work in your area.

You can offer the maps to tourists free by placing them in logical locations where the tourists will go.

Tutoring

Type: Part time
Startup costs: Low
Location: Student's home or at your home

Provide tutoring for students in a specific subject. Make sure you have the textbooks the students are using in their classes. Check out what it takes to be an approved tutor for sick students who cannot attend school.

Check out the home schooling sector to see if you can support their needs in more advanced subjects that the parents may not feel comfortable teaching.

This will require traditional media advertisement.

Utility Auditor

Type: Part time
Startup costs: Minimal
Location: Home based

People frequently don't understand their electric, gas, phone and water bills. There is an entire industry devoted to understanding how these companies should be billing residences and small businesses and making sure that the customers who hire the consultants are being billed fairly and at the lowest rate possible.

Frequently, the auditor will have to monitor the time-of-day usage to make sure a business client is getting the best rates for the time the service is used. Off-peak hour usage can be much cheaper for some utilities.

There are books and a lot of information on this subject available on the Internet. The first few jobs that you do will take a lot of learning and time. Then when you know the system, the reviews can be completed quickly.

You will have to do a lot of traditional advertising and direct mailings to gain customers. Payment is frequently based on a percent of the first year savings to the customer.

Valentine Day stores

Type: Seasonal
Startup costs: Low
Location: Rent a vacant retail storefront

Businesses take 1-month leases on vacant retail properties to sell gifts, roses and candy just for this holiday. To avoid longer-term leases, you will have to go where the building vacancies are and be ready to move out with only a few weeks notice.

Find a busy location where you can put up a big banner so you can minimize traditional advertising.

Vending routes

Type: Part time
Startup costs: High
Location: Home based

Earlier in the book, I warned you to stay away from the commercial sector of this business selling food and beverage items. They involve a lot of heavy lifting and many times big companies have a significant cost advantage. Try to focus on gumballs in those $.25 machines and other products that are lighter and have a much longer shelf life. Think about captive audiences wanting specific products such as toiletries at hotels, hygiene items in public restrooms or fishing bait and lures at boat launches. If you have a friend or relative that owns a place with a captive audience, utilize this relationship advantage.

While there are few DVD renting machines now, these will start popping up all over in a few years. You might consider putting them in hotels, college dorms, large apartment or condominium projects so you will not have to compete with all of the other video stores. You might also want to target your selection to a certain group or specific interest instead of trying to keep up with the new hits.

Videographer

Type: Hobby, part time
Startup costs: Medium
Location: Home based

Take the latest technology videos with top quality equipment. Serve special parties and events. Look into taking videos at corporate events and corporate customer's sales gatherings for mementos of the event. You will also need top quality editing equipment.

You might want to consider making high school sports videos for students to send to recruiters. Work with business people to put together video business cards so they can put a short presentation on a small DVD and use the label that has their normal business card information.

Advertise in local magazines catering to special events. Contact businesses directly if you are doing corporate events.

Water purification equipment

Type: Part time
Startup costs: Minimal
Location: Home office

In decades past, this business focus was on water softening equipment for areas that had hard water. We are seeing more areas with poor water quality that goes beyond what the kitchen sink filters can clean up. There are some growing franchises and distributorships for vendors that are selling whole-house water purification equipment.

Poor water quality will become more and more prevalent and this business sector will grow. The real magic in this industry is the continued maintenance and chemicals the equipment requires which is ongoing contacts for you.

You will have to do a lot of traditional advertisement to find your customers.

Web sales

Type: Part time
Startup costs: Low or medium
Location: Home based

People are selling items on the Internet. Some set up their own website while others use auctions sites. Some people stock items while others have the manufacturers or distributors drop ship the items directly to their customers. The possibilities are endless.

You may want to concentrate on a hobby of yours.

Getting located on the first page of many of the search engines is critical to your success if you have your own web site. Courses are offered through computer retailers on how to improve your placement with the search engines.

Wine tasting

Type: Part time
Startup costs: Low
Location: Home based

Offer wine tasting parties for charities and not-for-profit groups. Charge for the tasting itself so you break even and cash in on sales of your wine selections if that is allowed in your state.

Some wine stores do this currently as part of their business. In most states you will need to have your own liquor license or work through a liquor store for the sales.

Wine Tours

Type: Part time
Startup costs: Low
Location: Home based

In many parts of the country, there are areas that grow the grapes and wineries that make the wine. California's Napa Valley is just one of many. Tours of numerous wineries are great tourist attractions and great weekend adventures for the locals. The problem with these tours is driving after all those tastings.

One great idea is to get a group together and rent a limousine or bus so no one has to miss all of the tastings. You can offer these transportation services. Better yet, set up a tour with great locally known lunch and dinner stops and possibly a great bed and breakfast for the overnight stay. If the area is big enough, you can plan a multi-day tour.

Advertise locally in tourist publications or align with some charitable organizations to market through them. Advertise in tourist information guides.

Winter motorized equipment rental

Type: Seasonal
Startup costs: High
Location: Find an outdoor location where this equipment can be used and rent a lodge there or bring an RV to operate from

Rent out snowmobile equipment if you can find a location along the many paths that allow this equipment. Watch your insurance coverage and your liability for accidents. If you have the right property, you could have them come to your location for use.

Advertising in the local media will be needed to attract customers to your location.

Winter recreational equipment rentals

Type: Seasonal
Startup costs: Medium
Location: A local park

Rent out downhill skis, cross country skis, snow shoes, or snow tubing equipment at your favorite park, if allowed, or just outside the park entrance. Start small out of your truck using equipment you have bought at garage sales.

Location may give you a captive audience but you may need to advertise to get the customers there.

Wood-lot management

Type: Part time
Startup costs: Don't even consider this unless you already own the right property.
Location: Home based

There are many places in this country where hardwood trees grow. If you have large acreage in one of these areas, you might have a good suspicion that the trees you have are worth good money. The best way to find their value, to find someone to harvest them and to manage the harvesting so it will last through your retirement years is to hire a professional forestry consultant. Property owners will see this as a passive cash flow from their land.

About the author

Stan Spector is a merger & acquisitions specialist working with family owned businesses that want to cash out, enhance natural growth through acquisitions, or develop a new business model to find a **sustainable competitive advantage**. Working with these businesses has shown him how to develop successful part-time businesses to compete with low profit full-time businesses in the same sector.

He presents seminars for financial planners and other organizations working with baby boomers to try to instill the entrepreneurial spirit to overcome shortfalls in retirement savings. He can be contacted through his web site StanSpector.com.

He works with other seniors to help them find enjoyable businesses to enhance their "purpose" in their golden years.

A newsletter will be started through his web site that will provide user feedback on the businesses inspired by this book.